SPY INTERROGATIONS LEAD TO INVESTIGATIVE
REPORTING - A FADING ART

CONTENTS

1. IN DEPTH NEWS EROSION HELPED INSPIRE THIS VERY BOOK

2. HOW FAMILY LIFE EVER OVER TIME LEADS TO DOMINATING LIFE INTERESTS

3. MILITARY INVESTIGATIVE EXPERIENCES HELPED INSPIRE A CAREER IN NEWS REPORTING

4. THE DANGERS AND CHALLENGES OF INVESTIGATIVE REPORTING

5. DEVELOPMENTS HARMING INVESTIGATIVE REPORTERS

6. LIFE EXPERIENCES LEADING TO MY OWN INVESTIGATIVE REPORTING

7. THREATS AND CHALLENGES TO MY CAREER

8. CONNECTICUT CONTRACTORS USED PHONY MINORITY COMPANIES TO CHEAT A LAW BENEFITING ACTUAL MINORITY FIRMS

9. CORRUPTION SPREADS OVER THE YEARS IN HARTFORD PROBATE COURT

10. UGLY PRISON CONDITIONS INSPIRE IN DEPTH PROBE

11. INDIAN TRIBE OVERWHELMED BY CORRUPTION

12. TRASH HAULING BUSINESSES LINKED TO THE MAFIA

13. WILD BIRDS ARE MY ALL-TIME FAVORITE CREATURES

14. THE GULF WAR

15. ANTHRAX VACCINE CREATES INCREDIBLE HEALTH PROBLEMS DURING AND AFTER THE GULF WAR

16. PRESIDENT GEORGE BUSH TAKES US TO WAR

17. GOVERNMENT CORRUPTION REQUIRES TOUGH JOURNALISM WORLDWIDE TO HELP CONTROL IT

PREFACE

I was inspired to write this book after a career as an investigative reporter for The Hartford Courant for more than four decades and then afterward as a freelance newsman. Once I started writing, I couldn't stop. It was simultaneously the most difficult, yet inspiring tasks of my life. Editors, news sources and subjects constantly looked over my shoulder. Fortunately, I was only sued once for liable and ultimately after endless, aggravating days at trial, the newspaper, three of my news sources and I won. Only I researched and wrote that story after months of investigation. That made probes much more intense and nerve wracking than when I worked with wondrous news investigative reporters as partners and full witnesses to the day-by-day interviews and lengthy research. This book is also an autobiographical explanation highlighting scores of inspirations which led to my investigative career in journalism.

CHAPTER 1

In Depth News Erosion Helped Inspire This Very Book

Most news stories are usually read one day and tossed the next to be forgotten. The exceptions arrive when those articles are rare and deep investigative pieces, demanding more reading attention; or when reporters create gripping features a reader is compelled to pass on to friends and relatives. This is partly why my own life experiences led me to eventually become an investigative reporter for decades.

And my news probes we so intoxicating that I developed into a freelance investigative newsman after retiring from my almost four decades long career at The Hartford Courant.

However, then, unfortunately for me I ultimately retired from all my in-depth reporting work before I might have had the opportunity to somehow become involved in investigating and writing about one of the biggest scandals in U.S. history. That perpetual scorcher, of course, arose during the period before and after Donald Trump became president the United States in January 2017. It was such a relief when he lost in 2020, but of course, Trump refused to admit defeat even up to the point of Joe Biden, his opponent's confirmation in January 2021!

Within the last two and a half decades, newspaper ownerships constantly emphasized the deadly negatives: profits and their loyal readers are declining. Those perpetual eye opener adverse developments arose and continue as the Internet and discouraged and younger newspaper readers move life away from daily newspaper subscriptions, newsstands and even some Internet newspaper subscriptions.

My emotional concerns about that decline of journalism inspired me to write not only this book, but as well, an in depth news story about that very negative subject in 2006. It was just a year after I retired from those decades of work as a Hartford Courant reporter and began my freelance investigative reporting work. See [The Decline Of Journalism](#)

To quote the lead paragraph in that very article: "If some doomsday industry analysts are to be believed, newspapers are laid out and stacked neatly inside their own future death warehouses, not only in the United States, but worldwide."

Voila!!! After the Courant's decades long competitor, The Hartford Times, died, I could not resist accepting a speech to honor its passing.

Here is what The Tribune Business News reported on October 23, 2006, the year after my Courant retirement:

"Former Courant reporter Thomas D. (Dennie) Williams, who retired after 40 years in 2005, was the local news opponent Hartford Times reunion's keynote speaker. Williams recalled the pressure Times and Courant reporters operated under when Hartford was a two-newspaper town. 'I still remember how painful it was to be scooped by the Times,' Williams said, 'and how good it felt to scoop their reporters!

"Williams said that after the Times went out of business, the Courant lost some of its sense of urgency. "It wasn't the same afterward,' Williams said. 'Investigative pieces took longer to get into the paper because there was no competition anymore.' "

Now, instead of subscribing to newspapers, some rabid news fans regularly listen to largely superficial news on television, radio and anywhere on the Internet they can find it, especially including Google and Facebook. Yet both those powerful international Internet sites have faced strong critiques for producing inaccurate or false news reports, some of which may have impacted upon the outcome of the controversial 2016 presidential election. See Fake News in U.S. Election? Elsewhere, That's Nothing New (Published 2016)

Here is Media Matters definition of fake news and if you'd like more details, click on the Internet address below:

"While reporting real news requires a newsroom and some sort of process that can be critiqued and examined, "fake news" is built to obfuscate and hide sources. Its creators are varied, from a random American making $10,000 a month from his fabricated Facebook posts to a group of teenagers in Macedonia running more than a hundred pro-(Donald) Trump websites (assisting his victory over Hillary Clinton). (This phony) business model is simple: identify the news that people want to read, and give it to them, regardless of the truth and with no effort whatsoever put into actual reporting."

"There is no question that fake news got lots of attention in 2016, in part because the president-elect himself -- and several people close to him -- pushed fabricated information. That's deeply concerning, because data shows that not only do Americans believe lies they see on Facebook, but also that Americans across party lines say fake news is a real problem."

See: Misinformer Of The Year: The Ecosystem Of Fake News And The "Alt-Right"

A dramatic and shocking more recent example of cursory news was the 2016 presidential election. The two major party candidates, Hillary Clinton and Donald Trump, created numerous scandalous controversies about one another, prompting scores of daily news articles. But, overall nationwide, relatively few timely in depth or investigative pieces appeared to effectively help scans of voters clarify scurrilous circumstances, charges and counter charges.

Can anyone imagine what would have happened had an investigative piece with wide circulation appeared in a newspaper BEFORE the election about Trump's scandalous sexual behaviors with at least two women?

Other series of unrelated in-depth probes, largely from The New York Times and The Washington Post, largely became most intense AFTER Trump was elected president in November 2016.

After his win, President Trump seemed to even dream about restraining in depth and investigative reporting probing his alleged tight before and after election connections to Russian President Vladimir Putin and the Russia's massive illegal sneak blog support for Trump.

In early October 2017, MSNBC quoted the president as saying, ''Why Isn't the Senate Intel Committee looking into the Fake News Networks in OUR country to see why so much of our news is just made up-FAKE!" And he texted at one point, eight months earlier, in February 2017: "THE FAKE NEWS media (failing NY Times, CNN, NBC news and many more) is not my enemy, it is the enemy of the American people. SICK!"

But when January 2019 came along, President Trump indeed became closely tied to a series of confidential conversations with Putin.

"A Washington Post exclusive revealed: Citing 'current and former U.S. officials,' the Post reports President Trump has a 'pattern' of hiding those (Putin) conversations from government officials and that he has, at least once, taken his interpreter's notes and told them not to discuss a conversation with administration officials.

These actions have reportedly led to a lack of details about five of the president's face-to-face communications with Putin over the last two years." https://www.newsy.com/stories/washington-post-trump-hid-details-of-putin-conversations/
As reported in EAWorldview, here is part of that very situation:

"After a one-on-one session with Putin at the G20 summit in Germany in July 2017, Trump took the notes of his interpreter and instructed that very person not to discuss the encounter with other Administration officials. The officials learned of Trump's order when a White House adviser and a senior State Department official sought information from the interpreter beyond a readout from Secretary of State Rex Tillerson.

US officials said there is no detailed record, even in classified files, of Trump's face-to-face interactions with Putin at five locations over the past two years."

But even as much as revealing is this subsequent volunteer admission in The New York Times January 20, 2019 edition from Trump's well-known spokesman-attorney: "President Trump was involved in discussions to build a skyscraper in Moscow throughout the entire 2016 presidential campaign, his personal lawyer said on Sunday, a longer and more significant role for Mr. Trump than he had previously acknowledged."

The comments by his lawyer Rudolph W. Giuliani indicated that Mr. Trump's efforts to complete a business deal in Russia waned only after Americans cast ballots in the presidential election.

The new timetable means that Mr. Trump was seeking a deal at the time he was calling for an end to economic sanctions against Russia imposed by the Obama administration. He was seeking a deal when he gave interviews questioning the legitimacy of NATO, a favorite talking point of Russian President Putin. And he was seeking a deal when, in July 2016, he called on Russia to release hacked Democratic emails that Mr. Putin's government was rumored at the time to have stolen.

Meanwhile then, reportedly, U.S. Special Counsel Robert S. Mueller III was seeking witnesses to these sensationally controversial confidential conversations with Putin, some of which were covered up by Trump's seizing of the minutes.

Other of those conversations were not recorded or texted into minutes available to U.S officials. They have led to speculation that Trump is somehow under Putin's control as a result of his overwhelming approval of his and Russia's controversial international policies, mostly directly opposed to U.S. policies.

Trump's intensive critiques of the press, excluding his long-time favorite biased Fox News, has continued from day one of his life in the media going back to his days in business and continuing overwhelmingly ever since.

Back in October 2016, The Washington Post quoted Trump as claiming: "Our press is allowed to say whatever they want and get away with it. And I think we should go to a system where if they do something wrong, I'm a big believer, tremendous believer of the freedom of the press. Nobody believes that stronger than me. But, if they make terrible, terrible mistakes and those mistakes are made on purpose to injure people, and I'm not just talking about me, I'm talking about anybody else, then yes, I think you should have the ability to sue them."

Indeed, Trump wanted stricter libel laws like those in England.

"Well in England they have a system where you can actually sue if someone says something wrong," Trump said. "Our press is allowed to say whatever they want and get away with it. And I think we should go to a system where if they do something wrong -- I'm a big believer, tremendous believer of the freedom of the press, nobody believes it stronger than me -- but if they make terrible, terrible mistakes and those mistakes are made on purpose to injure people, and I'm not just talking about me, I'm talking about anybody else, then yes, I think you should have the ability to sue them."
See CNN Business News: [Donald Trump says he wants libel laws more like the UK's](#)

Trump wanted to change the libel law for politicians like him. The Digital Media Law Project says, that law is stricter for "celebrities, politicians, high-ranking or powerful government officials, and others with power in society (because they) are generally considered public figures/officials and are required to prove actual malice. On the other hand, a private figure is only required to prove negligence if you publish something defamatory about (them)."

Controversial in depth and investigative stories often appeared late in the 2016 presidential contest. They were delayed enough that their impact on opposing candidates and the public, and even more important, undecided voters, came too late for intelligent decision-making. The national press reported a number of in-depth exposes, critiquing Mr. Trump, but the many of the most effective and powerful ones appeared AFTER he won the primaries and the presidency.

The controversial probe of Trump for his and his election promotional team began in May 2017 after allegations surfaced that they were suspected of teaming with the Russians to influence the presidential election on his behalf.

Here is the Wikipedia summary of it: "The ongoing Special Counsel investigation is a United States law enforcement and counterintelligence investigation of any Russian government efforts to interfere in the 2016 presidential election, including an investigation of any possible links and/or coordination between Donald Trump's presidential campaign and the Russian government, 'and any matters that arose or may arise directly from the investigation.'

"The scope of the investigation reportedly also includes potential obstruction of justice by Trump and others. The investigation, since it began May 17, 2017, has been conducted by the United States Department of Justice Office of Special Counsel, headed Mueller, a former Director of the Federal Bureau of Investigation (FBI). Mueller took over several existing FBI investigations, including those involving former campaign chairman Paul Manafort and former National Security Adviser Michael Flynn."

That investigation has resulted in dozens of indictments for federal crimes, including charges leading to guilty pleas by Manafort and Flynn who have since agreed to cooperate with Mueller's and his team's investigation along with other crucial witnesses who also have been charged and plead guilty. The probes of Trump, himself, have worked closer and closer to Mueller's obvious but confidential aims at implicating the president himself.

The most controversial of scores of investigations pointing to possible Trump criminal activities came in February 2019. That was when his former lawyer-confidant Michael Cohen began more of his testimony in Congress and supplied checks used for payments of Trump's sexual activity with Stormy Daniels, an adult film porn star.

The investigative effort was aimed at possibly leading Mueller to refer Trump to the U.S. House of Representatives for an investigation, which if concluded unfavorably for him, would move Trump on to a trial in U.S. Senate. It would require two thirds of the senators' votes to remove him from office.

On Friday the 13th of December, 2019, the House Judiciary Committee approved two articles of impeachment against Donald Trump for abusing power in his dealings with Ukraine and obstructing Congress in their investigation of those actions, passed almost exclusively along party lines,

After a 14-hour hearing, the committee voted 23-17, along party lines, to recommend to the House that Trump be impeached for abuse of power and obstruction of Congress. But, after that in February 2020, the Senate voted to acquit President Trump on impeachment charges of abuse of power and obstruction of Congress over his dealings with Ukraine, marking the end of the months-long saga that dominated Washington.

Throughout his four years of the presidency, Trump's incredible fights with political disputes continued right through his controversial competition with his Democratic political presidential opponent, Joseph Biden in 2020. But in that battle, which Biden formally won in November of the very year, after continuous national vote counts, the battle continued. Trump initially said he was going to regain the presidency by legally challenging the vote counts. But that effort failed, and Trump continued his fight seemingly endlessly before it ended. In that end, Biden took over the job as required in January 202!

Today, the comparatively increasing lack of timely four-dimensional news, with one obvious exception being investigations of Trump for his prior to office corruption, erodes the crucial and historical civic need for what used to be more frequently known as The Fourth Estate. Certainly, news sites now are more concerned about expenses than they were. Those concerns most obviously began reduction of news expenses in the late 1990s and early 2000s to especially diminish and curtail time consuming investigative reporting.

In some newspapers, the reduction of in-depth Biden reporting led to less and less substantial news and in depth reporting as well. That helped develop a lack of substantial news values among news reporters and editors and certainly helped eventual development of one dimensional as well as fake news.

This is an excellent Media Matters story by John **Whitehouse** (!) about how it is to be fake and not fake inside the news. Misinformer HYPERLINK "https://www.mediamatters.org/tucker-carlson/misinformer-year-ecosystem-fake-news-and-alt-right" Of The Year: The Ecosystem Of Fake News And The "Alt-Right" | Media Matters for America

US News and World Report explains: "…as trust in the mainstream media has eroded and use of social media as a news source has risen, fake news may have become more influential than ever before, wrote Rachel Dicker, Newsday's Associate Editor of Social Media. "Millions of people read and share fake news or propaganda on social media without even knowing it."

Vox asked Facebook CEO Mark Zuckerberg about fake news. The news site reported Zuckerberg's essential point: "Facebook will look for new ways to stop the spread of fake news, but he also argues that 'we must precede very carefully' and Facebook must be 'extremely cautious about becoming arbiters of truth ourselves.'
"See Facebook's fake news problem, explained

The American Press Institute even lays out intelligent and basic questions for anxious and troubled news primers and readers "that will tell you who to trust." The underlying quiz: "What kind of content is this? Who and what are the sources cited and why should I believe them? What's the evidence (of trust) and how was it vetted? Is the main point of the piece proven by the evidence? Completeness: What's missing? Am I learning every day what I need (to know)?"

That Institute gives "Six questions that will tell you what media to trust....How do you know what to trust? Ask these six questions and they will unlock whether something is trustworthy."
HERE THEY ARE DIRECTLY QUOTED
FROM https://www.americanpressinstitute.org/publications/six-critical-questions-can-use-evaluate-media-content
1. Type: What kind of content is this?

2. Source: Who and what are the sources cited and why should I believe them?
3. Evidence: What's the evidence and how was it vetted?
4. Interpretation: Is the main point of the piece proven by the evidence?
5. Completeness: What's missing?
6. Knowledge: Am I learning every day what I need?

This gives the concerned reader why these crucial queries are essential for caring reporters and newsreaders. As a result of their fiscal troubles, for years, newspaper publishers have been searching ways to cut back drastically on the expense and space needed for news subjects which demanded much time and more expensive talent.

How can papers do that without losing readers and, as well, in depth or even accurate news? Nonetheless, as an expense-slash result, a host of papers have been laying off experienced, capable reporters, who attract sophisticated readers demanding accuracy.

Many publishers' last priority today is spending money for experienced reporters' higher salaries or expensive long range investigations. Instead, they push hard for daily news and inexpensive features, as well as scandals handed to reporters by law enforcement news releases or other, sometimes questionable, sources. And many newspapers are relying on wire reports for crucial stories rather than their own sincere news reporting work.

These publishers and editors are eliminating the very news staffers having strong ambitions, curiosity and patience to uncover a myriad of corrupt activities which have failed to be pursued by local and state police, the FBI and other government investigators.

Such in depth news reporting requires "a low threshold, anger about things that you've seen and believe are unfair, unjust or hypocritical, or in some way or another violating public trust," says Pulitzer-winning James Steele, a Philadelphia Inquirer reporter.
See http://spectator.sme.sk/c/20062208/this-is-the-golden-age-of-access.html

Eroding journalistic developments and values are extremely discouraging to enterprising editors and reporters. Some publishers nationwide, seeking profits above integrity, have eliminated news staff with the strong ambitions, curiosity and the patience to uncover the myriad of corrupt activities.

Fortunately, there are national and international news organizations still focusing on widespread local and worldwide corruption. For instance, writes Wikipedia, The International Consortium of Investigative Journalists is "a Washington-based international network (was) launched in 1997 by the Center for Public Integrity." It "includes 165 investigative journalists in over 65 countries who work together on issues such as 'cross-border crime, corruption, and the accountability of power...' See: International Consortium of Investigative Journalists

But, notwithstanding some amazing worldwide news organizations, like those mentioned in Wikipedia, all countries obviously need to have regular daily and monthly news organizations to expose the often disguised and underrated dirty and ugly activities of corporate and government officials as well as the Mafia and just plain ordinary, but powerful crooks.

In Mexico, those professional criminals can cobble together in various ways to control whole areas of the country. Here is what the story Mexican Profile says inside.

"Mexico is home to the hemisphere's largest, most sophisticated and violent organized criminal groups. These organizations have drawn from Mexico's long history of smuggling and its close proximity to the United States, the world's largest economy, to grow into a regional threat. Their networks stretch from Argentina to Canada and even into Europe.

They traffic in illegal drugs, contraband, arms and humans, and launder their proceeds through regional money changers, banks and local economic projects," says InsightCrime. See: Mexico organized crime news (insightcrime.org)

With all this criminal activity needed for coverage by daily news reporters, specialized police reporters, or those now relatively few investigating corruptions in depth, journalists are facing serious criminal victim threats themselves! The Committee to Protect Journalists estimates that 1,236 journalists have been killed since 1992. At least 804 of those killings were classified as murders, 274 as combat cross fires and 154 as a result of dangerous assignments,

On April 29, 2017, Azam Ahmed The New York Times staffer reported that it has "Become Easy to Kill a Journalist in a Mexican State." In particular Ahmed said that "the Mexican State of Veracruz is the most dangerous place to be a reporter in the entire Western Hemisphere." That, he writes, is due to out of control drug mobsters and even corrupt government officials who want to make journalists pay for their dangerous news exposures of the area's uncontrolled crime.

'Mexico is one of the worst countries in the world to be a journalist today. At least 104 journalists have been murdered in this country since 2000, while 25 others have disappeared (and are) presumed dead," writes Mr. Azam.

That figure is much higher than the one published by The Committee to Protect Journalists'. It says 37 Mexican journalists have been murdered and three more were killed as a result of dangerous assignments since 1992.

"During the 2008–09 recession, submissions to the popular Investigative Reporters and Editors contest dropped 34.1 percent compared to 2006–07, indicating the extent of the cutback," writes Jack Shafer from the April 2017 in the April 2017 issue of Reason.

In the United States, going back decades, this fourth dimension was inspired by veteran news editors and reporters, closely monitoring irregularities in governments and businesses.

They naturally did so to expose the frequently ignored corruption, irregular activities and law breaking among overly powerful politicians and millionaire, now billionaire, tycoons.

Corruption can be widespread as well within the educational system, religious elite and labor unions. In those worlds, powerful administrators, church leaders and union officials create their own brand of immoral or illegal environments. Newsmen and women with such topic specialties still, as they used to, absolutely need to blow their whistles on even Popes as well as university presidents or union stewards and chiefs, controversial drug makers, lawyers and doctors.

Investigative news stories can indeed have impacts, inspiring necessary government and business policy changes and clean ups. One particularly dramatic and historical example of that news need was produced by the outstanding series of articles exposing the Watergate Scandal. That award-winning journalism was accomplished by veteran Washington Post reporters Bob Woodward and Carl Bernstein, during President Richard Nixon's administration.

Bernstein and Woodward were called in to work on that huge Watergate Scandal in the summer of 1972. Two years later, In August 1974, their amazing well-researched investigative pieces helped lead to the ultimate removal of Nixon from government. He was forced to resign, but his successor, Gerald Ford pardoned Nixon for all the crimes he "committed or may have committed" while in office, says a history of the scandal. See at The Watergate Scandal - Timeline, Summary HYPERLINK "https://www.history.com/topics/1970s/watergate"& HYPERLINK "https://www.history.com/topics/1970s/watergate" Deep Throat - HISTORY

So sometimes, even the finest news reporting, although creating crucial action like official resignation, cannot induce the fullest of best results.

What follows is a succinct explanation of the contrast between the news values that used to be, during Watergate, and those of today from The Global Watchdog Media Accountability Coalition.

"If it were left to me to decide whether we should have a government without a free press or a free press without a government, I would prefer the latter," said Thomas Jefferson. I wonder if Jefferson would feel the same after an hour of watching shouting heads screaming at each other on today's infotainment that purports to be news."

"Edward R. Murrow was perhaps one of the most important reasons the nation turned against Senator McCarthy and his witch hunts. When Walter Cronkite began to sour on the war in Vietnam the sentiment of the nation began to shift. President Lyndon Johnson, watching live in the White House, reportedly said, "If I've lost Cronkite, I've lost Middle America." Global Watchdog details this threat. See [Georgia medical marijuana commission looking for growers, manufacturers | News Break](#)

Today with news erosion, it is hard to believe, particularly, that Popes and Bishops, not just priests, were exposed years back by reporting focused on serious irregularities. Check out my former Hartford Courant reporting colleague Gerald Renner's and his co-author. Jason Berry's book, Vows of Silence: The Abuse of Power in the Papacy of John Paul II. It was based on their long hard newspaper inquiry work creating investigative story after story earlier. Berry, who worked for The Legionaries of Christ, teamed with The Courant's Renner in crucial 1997 Courant news inquiry articles.

From the 1960s to the 1990s, this news reporter, as well as that wondrous "Gerry" Renner, now deceased, and others were fortunate enough to have orchestrated scores of in-depth probes. Why? That four-dimensional news was then the culture not only in The Courant, but many newspapers nation-wide.

Renner and his reporting partner, Berry, exposed the Catholic leadership, including two Popes for allowing Father Marcial Maciel

Degollado, the founder of the ultraconservative Legion of Christ, to sexually abuse "more than 20 and less than 100 victims." The Legion is a Mexican Roman Catholic religious institute, made up of priests and seminarian studying for the priesthood.

Renner's and Berry's incredible investigative news efforts back in 1997, went unrecognized in the media when the Boston Globe took on a similar Popal scandal news series winning them a Pulitzer Prize in 2003. The background coverage of the Globe's stories by that paper and others made it sound like The Courant's stories exposing those very same extra sexual sandal problems with priests and others inside the church had never existed.

CHAPTER 2

HOW FAMILY LIFE OVER TIME LEADS TO DOMINATING LIFE INTERESTS

Growing up, I was fortunate to have both a mother, Constance Ripley, and a father, Thomas, Williams, who through their own remarkable talents, taught me to face challenges.

Mom inspired me indirectly through her own experience as an artist in the theater, while Dad sparked an interest in the news with his overwhelming fascination for local and national politics and constant reading of the news and news columns penned by talented journalists.

Before she married Dad in the 1930s, Mom, then Constance Ripley, became well known on and off Broadway as a talented fashion and costume designer for many famous actors and actresses. They included Jimmy Durante, Bob Hope, Ethel Merman, Katharine Hepburn, as well as Fred and Adele Astaire.

A member of the song writers Hall of Fame, Cole Porter, was one of several composers arranging music for her plays, including the stage musical Red Hot And Blue. Constance Ripley worked for seven years with famous Broadway designer Norman Bel Geddes. He did scenic designs for the Metropolitan Opera and designed, produced, or directed some 200 operas, films, plays, and musical comedies. See: https://www.britannica.com/biography/Norman-Bel-Geddes

Here above is a wondrous example of Ms. Ripley's costumes in an exhibition of her work.

Before they were married, Dad used to attend some of the play previews. One day, a star comic was being replaced temporarily by his understudy, because the famed comic was not feeling well. But he was present behind the curtain.

Dad had a loud laugh, and when the replacement was acting out his part, Dad started laughing and did so repeatedly. A loud laugh echoes throughout an empty theater. When this preview ended, the star comic burst out from behind the curtain and on to the stage. He exclaimed loudly, "I want him (his amusing under study) eliminated as my replacement for this play!" In one of the most famous of her costume plays, The Bandwagon, here is a wondrous dress!

The wonderful dress is worn by Tillie Losch, who starred in the play with Fred Astaire, Adele Astaire and Helen Broderick.

And, here is a dramatic description of Mom's costumes from a December 8th, 1934, New Yorker Magazine review of another famous Broadway play, the musical comedy, "Revenge With Music."

"One of the reasons why "Revenge With Music" seemed so different from the general run of foot-stampings and teeth-flashings and head-tossing is the remarkable effects with subdued colors which Constance Ripley has managed to get into costumes.

There are rich browns and purples and dull yellows, but there isn't a Spanish shawl, as we have come to know, Spanish shawls, in the place. I distinctly remember one entire ensemble in which the only touch of bright red was at the throat of one of the women. I must have been in one of my more aesthetic moods, for I was acutely color-conscious throughout the evening and on the point of swooning several times. You don't suppose, do you, that at my age I am starting to react to color schemes?"

There was however another actress, I remember Mother telling me, in another play, that was not as pleased as Tillie was with her costume.

Katharine Hepburn, who my mother told me was readying for a rehearsal, became so upset with the dress my mother had designed that she ripped it up and threw it at her. That was a once in a lifetime experience for my Mom!

When she sketched her designs, she used several different mediums: pencil and water color, pen and ink, pen and water color, charcoal and colored pencil and some air brush or atomizer.

Here are some of the well-known plays for which she produced costumes:

Red, Hot and Blue [Original, Musical, Comedy]

Oct 29, 1936 - Apr 10, 1937

Parade [Original, Musical, Revue, Satire]

May 20, 1935 - Jun 22, 1935

Revenge with Music [Original, Musical]

Nov 28, 1934 - Apr 27, 1935

Flying Colors [Original, Musical, Revue]

Sep 15, 1932 - Jan 25, 1933

The Cat and the Fiddle [Original, Musical, Romantic Comedy]

Oct 15, 1931 - Sep 24, 1932

The Band Wagon [Original, Musical, Revue]

Jun 3, 1931 - Jan 16, 1932

Dad, a Yale University graduate, read as many as three newspapers a day and was a skilled letter writer, as well as a man with a strong interest in national and local politics. Almost any time he read about corruption in any government world-wide he was compelled to talk about it!

That is a trait I began sharing, even early in my life. Dad was the Democratic Town Chairman for the Town of Litchfield, Connecticut, and once ran unsuccessfully for first selectman. He had an outgoing personality with a charming sense of humor. A few of his early jobs demanded salesmanship, a quality Dad had plenty of.

Eventually, Mom's and Dad's artistic and personal interests melded, and they became famous in the New England area as American antique dealers, selling rare paintings, furniture and American pewter. That required extensive research into art and historical topics. Dad, more than Mom, constantly talked about those very subjects. But Mom constantly inspired Dad, their customers and show participants about the rarity and beauty of centuries-old art, pottery and furniture. Here are those dealer partners relaxing at home below

Here's what Antiques and The Arts Weekly says about them: "At the end of the alphabet and rounding up the Salisbury Antiques Fair list of exhibitors was Thomas C. & Constance R. Williams, the famous pewter people of Litchfield, Conn. Yes, Williams and pewter were one and the same, but their interests in antiques ran in many directions, including paintings, furniture and rugs. And they were always ready to talk about antiques, to share their knowledge, be it at a small show around the corner from home or at their front booth at the Winter Antiques Show."

My past dreams of Mom and Dad are related to Mom's theater days that they occasionally described to me and playing golf with Dad and his lifelong close friend John Winslow, whom I called Uncle Snead.

Impossible! Two Wonderful Dreams In A Row!

Perhaps these dreams were somewhat inspired by my mother, a costume designer in the theater and my Dad who loved to play golf at the Litchfield Country Club.

Last night, I was sleeping so tight that I had no idea I was in dream land. Suddenly, I was sitting in the front row watching a wonderful musical play. My seat was level with the stage…so level I could see the actors and actresses shiny brown and black shoes rushing or walking or flying by. I was absolutely mesmerized!

Their costumes were all very bright but different shades of reds, greens and yellows. But the brightness of their clothes looked like the solid colors viewed in a sharp caricature painting, although not as totally realistic as the lively players.

It was a play that I thought I had seen somewhere else years earlier; the actors and actresses seemed to know me by sight. One or two or three, put their feet out as if to touch me while continuing to walk by, while other dancers kicked out their pointed shoes in my direction so close I almost had to flinch.

The stage seemed twice as long as ones I had seen before on Broadway. I kept being hypnotized while my brain nevertheless kept trying to remember the name of this wonderful musical. I couldn't! Suddenly, a loud alarm went off, and awakened me. I was in immediate shock and so extremely disappointed, so much so that I am still trying to remember the name of the play and the identities of the actors and actresses who seemed to somehow know me.

A night earlier, I was again in a deep sleep when suddenly I was out walking near part of the little Bantam River on the Litchfield Golf Course where I had played golf numerous times when I was much younger.

I had stopped to hang around a group of three or four people I didn't even know. They weren't playing golf, just socializing on a cloudy afternoon. There was no way to play golf anyway because winter was turning to spring and ice spots were all over the fairways near the river which had overflowed and caused the banks to sag and erode.

As the talking continued, with me just listening nearby, a very attractive young lady suddenly broke through what used to be the river bank and disappeared from sight.

Everybody with her was so shocked; they seemed to freeze in place. I, however, rushed right to the spot where she disappeared and almost dove to the hole with my knees sliding to the ground. The young lady's arms and hands were reaching upwards in the dirty brown water.

Somehow, I grabbed them both and pulled her upwards to the ground. She was obviously soaking wet and somewhat in shock. The young lady choked the water out of her throat, and as she did I awoke in shock but with such relief. I will never, ever forget that dream.

JOHN AND JULIE FORMAN: THE BEST OF ALL LIFETIME INFLUENCES

Two of my other lifelong powerful influences were John and Julie Forman, shown above.

Aunt Julie was my mother's amazingly musically talented sister from the well-known Litchfield, Connecticut, Ripley family, whose forebearers lived there since the mid-1800s.

John, a good athlete, was the son of respected missionaries who taught school for decades in India. John's and Julie's integrity and religious faith overwhelmingly inspired those qualities on all the young students around them.

The Formans, then a relatively newly married couple, founded the Forman School in Litchfield in 1930 with three students who hadn't had a history of academic success in a traditional setting.

John emphasized Forman School's symbols in a 1956 graduation speech. "He underscored the significance of the lion as a symbol for moral courage, the green and white as representing growth and purity respectively. The gold, he said, stood for the greatest worth: character."

"Forman grew quickly and added a separate school for girls in 1942. The two schools formally merged in 1971. That school expanded over the years into a gateway to college for learning disabled students," says the school's Internet site. Starting with just a single house, Forman grew into a full campus.

I was a student at Forman School for five years. My sister, Connie, was a student there as well, but unlike me, she graduated from there and eventually went on to Barnard College in New York City. She constantly writes a variety of poems and has played a piano since she was a child.

Dr. Albert Einstein, who had faced reading challenges of his own as a student, joined the Forman School's Academic Board of Advisers and adding his input to the school's groundbreaking curriculum.

Beyond Einstein's influence, Julie and John, who were Christian Scientists, taught religion and imparted to their students wonderful moral values which, for those who paid attention, became implanted in their souls.

For me their teachings impressed on me the importance of attempting to have empathy for others, no matter how tough one's own life experiences were.

Aunt Julie and Uncle John not only furnished me with several years of inspiring teaching and playing of soccer, hockey and baseball, but outside of school, they stimulated Connie, Mom, Dad and I with wondrous experiences in nature.

They drove, walked and explored with us, particularly around their remote second homes in Banff, Canada and Barnard, Vermont, two rustic abodes set within pristine natural landscapes. They had a beautiful log cabin right next to the gorgeous Bow River in Banff, and later an A-frame overlooking the spectacular Green Mountains all the way north to Mt. Mansfield, the highest mountain in Vermont with a summit that peaks at 4,395 feet.

The Formans and the whole Williams family had so much fun checking out mountain ranges, lakes and rivers where we came across an amazing variety of birds, bears, other wildlife and forests. One sunny day in Banff, John sat outside and waited for the arrival of a baby deer and its mother. Amazingly, the wild Mom and Baby sidled right up to John and ate some carrots he had prepared to feed them! I can still remember that moment, welded in my mind close to six decades ago.

Not far away, the Williamses and the Formans experienced an arduous, but fun mountain adventure on horseback next to beautiful Lake Louise. The hardworking and experienced mountain climber horses took us miles up winding and steep cliffs to a gorgeous light blue pond adjacent to the nearby mountain top.

We explored on foot and even tried a little unsuccessful fishing before turning around for the trip downward. I was so frightened on the way down that I couldn't take any photos!

The mischievous horse seemed to desire safe spookiness for its rider. On endless turns around the winding course with unnerving, steep sinking views, the black creature leaned its neck outward, as if it wanted a faster course straight downward.

It seemed like the two of us would never complete that seemingly endless trip to the flats! Once we got to the lake area, I was so emotionally exhausted and welded to the horse's back that I needed help to get down to the snowy ground.

MORE FORMAN MEMORIES

Another personal tale that I will never forget, started with listening to the radio inside my Forman School bedroom and ended with a story in The Wall Street Journal years later.

I am a Giants' baseball fan and have been one since before their outfielder, Bobby Thompson, hit "the home run heard round the world" off Brooklyn Dodgers' pitcher Ralph Branca. That shot bouncing into the Polo Grounds crowded stands won the deciding third playoff game for the pennant in 1951.

The Giants had come from 13 1/2 games back to force that three-game playoff with the Dodgers. I was supposed to be studying at my desk inside my school room, but instead, I had the radio on softly and was listening intensively to every play in the game.

When Giants Radio Announcer Russ Hodges repeatedly screamed out "The Giants win the pennant" right after Bobby's winning home run, I leaped from my chair screaming in delight, hit my head against the low ceiling and dropped to the floor! Amidst the moaning, my screams continued. It was then the thrill of my 11-year-old life.

Later, I called my Dad, who made me into a loyal Giants' fan years earlier, and passionately asked: "Dad, did you hear the game on the radio?" He replied casually, "I listened, but turned it off in the last of the ninth before Bobby hit that amazing home run." When I exclaimed, "Dad, how could you do that?!" he replied, "You'll understand the pain of losing in the ninth when you get older!"

He was absolutely right! One day years later, when I was remotely listening to a tense Giants game from the kitchen, and it was on in the TV room, my son, Tommie, yelled out, "Dad, get in here, Will Clark is up for the Giants." I replied, "I can't! You'll understand why later!"

Clark was then the amazing star of the Giants team and later became a Giants' coach. I have to admit, I can't remember what happened so Will must have grounded out!

Now I remember a feature article on that Bobby Thompson home run years later in The Wall Street Journal. The writer described in detail the activities of the Giants' pitch sign stealer. He spied home plate with binoculars way out through a locker room window in center field, 505 feet away. There he regularly stole catchers' signs and relayed them immediately by signals through to home plate. That coach allegedly warned Bobby of a high fastball from Ralph, the one Thompson hit for that dramatic home run! Here is that alleged theft story.

See https://www.wsj.com/articles/SB980896446829227925

But I also remember most vividly that another article mentioned that after Bobby was mobbed at home plate, he went into the dugout, sat down and looked saddened. When another player was surprised and asked what was wrong, Bobby told him he was worried about how Ralph felt after throwing him the home run ball.

Bobby then explained that he felt like visiting Ralph to soothe his obvious grave upset. They later met up and became friends for the rest of their lives. I have never forgotten Bobby's rare thoughtfulness, as impressive to me as his season-winning home run!

Another personal memory and thrill of mine was sparked by a letter to me from my famous uncle, Sidney Dillon Ripley, former Secretary of The Smithsonian Institution, who knew I loved baseball. He wrote to me that the baseball legend, Hall of Famer, Charles Dillon "Casey" Stengel, was a cousin of ours. He added a photo of Casey as a player leaping for a baseball line drive. He had been both the manager of the Yankees and Mets.

Another memorable incident which is deeply etched into my mind took place early in my marriage when my wife Ina, myself and our two children, Gisela and Tommie, lived in a relatively small log cabin adjacent to the Ripley family's former home, which by then had become the Kilravock Inn. That inn was located in a monumental Tudor-style mansion, named after Kilravock Castle in Scotland. The original castle is located near the village of Croy, between Inverness and Nairn, in the council area of Highland, Scotland.

The Kilravock Inn tragically burned down on July 26, 1976. On that evening my family was visiting friends on the southern Connecticut shore near Rhode Island. I was outside on the porch, when suddenly my longtime friend, Hubert Santos, exclaimed through the open door: "Don't you own the Kilravock Inn?! It's burning down in a fire!"

In a state of shock, I hurried Ina and our two young children into a van and rushed home. When we arrived at Brush Hill Road, which led to our house, it was blocked off a quarter of a mile away from the inn.

We were forced to drive several miles to Knox Road so we could use that way to the inn. The shock viewing its continuing destruction was far too overwhelming, so we found a short way down the road to get home and had to live with nightmares before awaking the next morning to observe the devastating damage.

I spent an emotional day, going in and out of the wreckage to salvage furniture and other memorable and valuable antique goods.

As I was doing so, a guest on the night of blaze approached me as I was carrying furniture outside and my clothing was black from fire dust. She asked me if I was one of the inn's owners and I confirmed. Then, she emotionally informed me that as a guest she had a room on the second floor and lost all her jewelry from the fire. Immediately, she asked what I was going to do to compensate her.

I looked her directly in the eyes, fell silent but seconds later exclaimed: "Do you remember, by chance, what this amazing inn looked like before yesterday's fire?!" She replied, "Yes, it was amazing!" I answered immediately, "That's what I lost!" The conversation abruptly ended!

Here is what that Kilravock Inn looked like before and after the building burned down

Here below are images of Kilravock Castle in Croy, Scotland, which inspired Litchfield Kilravock's naming. The castle was built around 1460 and has been the seat of the Clan Rose since that time.

Years after that Kilravock Inn fire, Gisela Williams, my daughter, who became a freelance journalist, convinced me to go with her to the property's namesake castle to write a story for the Wall Street Journal on the castle's connection to my grandmother as a result of her Scottish upbringing. What a trip! Here is the story on the Internet:

By Gisela Williams The Wall Street Journal

A Custom Ancestry Tour in Scotland Experts who blend genealogy with travel can uncover your clan's history—and guide you through it, too

FOREBEARS FOUND | The writer traced her roots to Kilravock Castle in Scotland.

MY FATHER AND I were the only people eating in the dining room of Kilravock Castle in the Scottish Highlands—but we were hardly alone. The cream-papered walls were hung with portraits of former chiefs of the Rose clan. Several, with elaborate wigs and fleshy noses, stared disconcertingly down at us.

"I think I see a family resemblance," I said to Dad, only half joking.

Neither of us had been before to Kilravock, a stone manor built around a 15th-century fortified tower. (Bonnie Prince Charlie is said to have slept there in the 1740s and Cawdor Castle, mentioned in Shakespeare's "Macbeth," is a neighbor.) But we had heard about the place all our lives.

My father's mother, Constance Williams, wore scarves in the Rose family tartan. The Tudor-style mansion that her father and mother, Constance Bailey Rose, built in Litchfield, Conn., was dubbed Kilravock. Both women were named in honor of the Rose clan's motto: "Constant and True."

A Custom Ancestry Tour in Scotland

My father believed the family lore that we were direct descendants of the owners of Kilravock Castle. I, on the other hand, was skeptical. For his 70th birthday I hired a niche travel company, U.K.-based Ancestral Footsteps, to plan a trip to Scotland—and settle the castle question once and for all.

As producers for the BBC series "Who Do You Think You Are?" Sue Hills, owner of Ancestral Footsteps, and her employee, Jo Foster, investigated the family histories of celebrities like Jeremy Irons. Now they offer their services to regular folk, combining in-depth genealogical research with treasure-hunt-like journeys that reveal their findings, clue by clue, along the way.

"We liken it to a university dissertation or a commissioned portrait," Ms. Hills explained over the phone.

To keep costs down, I asked Ms. Hills to limit our expedition to three nights (two in a cottage on the grounds of Kilravock) and to focus on the castle and my great-grandmother, Constance Bailey Rose. Born in Canada to Scottish immigrants, she married well and, though her husband abandoned her, raised four overachieving children. My grandmother became a costume designer who worked with Fred and Adele Astaire; her brother Dillon was head of the Smithsonian Institution.

Eight months after I gave Ancestral Footsteps everything we had on Constance and the castle, my father and I landed in Edinburgh. The city was majestic but unexpectedly chilly, even for early May. We took a brisk walk up the Royal Mile to Edinburgh Castle, then retreated to the National Museum of Scotland to learn more about our ancestral homeland's history. As we wandered rooms filled with centuries-old weapons, we realized just how bloody and constant the local struggles for power had been—hence, the stone tower at the heart of Kilravock.

The next morning, Ms. Foster met us in the 18th-century building that houses the National Records of Scotland.

"There are endless Roses in the world, and thousands in the Scottish Highlands alone," she declared. "But only a few can trace their family line back to Kilravock."

Though she knew how our quest would end, she made us start at the beginning by looking up several dusty records (a birth certificate, a wedding contract, a will) that belonged to Constance Bailey's grandfather, the Rev. Lewis Rose. They revealed that my great-great-great-grandfather was born in 1791—not at the castle, which would have quickly confirmed our family connection, but on a farming estate nearby.

Run by a family of genealogists, Ancestral Attic specializes in Poland. The firm conducts research, finds living relatives and conducts private guided tours of areas where clients have roots. https://ancestralattic.com/

"Unfortunately, it seems the trail ends there," Ms. Foster said. "At least for today."

A chauffeured car took us into the raw, dramatic Highlands as Ms. Foster regaled us with stories of our headstrong ancestor. Rev. Rose had been involved in the Disruption of 1843, when 450 ministers left the Church of Scotland for the Free Church of Scotland, which rejected control by the state or aristocracy. He was relocated from Glasgow to the seaside village of Tain, to help prevent dissent from spreading.

The move was probably a disappointment for him—as Kilravock initially was for us. The castle was our first stop in the Highlands, and even as we pulled into its drive, we could see that the facade was crumbling. The inside was gloomy and cold, and calling it a "castle" was a stretch. Still, the notion that our ancestors had lived (and plotted) there was captivating.

The following morning we drove an hour or so to Tain, where we wandered among the moss-covered gravestones in the tiny cemetery of St. Duthac Church. In the historical society nearby, two women waited for us with a tattered book.

"It's an album of the villagers who lived here in the late 1800s," explained one, a volunteer for Tain Through Time. She carefully turned pages of sepia-toned photos until she reached one of a minister with wild gray hair and a severe expression. Rev. Rose bore a startling similarity to my father, and we became so engrossed in reading letters related to his battles with the town that we nearly forgot about the castle.

Just as well. Ms. Foster reminded us that a 1928 book of Church of Scotland ministers listed Rev. Rose's father, Alexander, as a "tacksman. That meant a landholder, one often related to the clan chief—but it was hardly a definitive link to Kilravock. At least where our family trail ended again, the whiskey trail began. We detoured to the renowned Glenmorangie distillery for a tour and tasting.

Love of whiskey may have been what drove the reverend's third son—Constance Bailey's father—to emigrate. In his early 30s he moved to London to become a spirits merchant. But Ms. Foster showed us a page from the Edinburgh Gazette from 1854, reporting that Lewis Rose had been sued by his creditor and his estate confiscated.

"Guess who was suing him?" she asked, pausing dramatically. "His own father, the reverend." Little wonder Canada had seemed appealing.

We stopped for tea at Lethen House, an 18th-century manse owned by local amateur historian Sarah Brodie. Ms. Foster had asked if Rev. Rose's father's farm appeared on the old maps piled in one of Ms. Brodie's libraries. It didn't, but other documents placed the property at a bend of the Nairn River.

Ms. Foster led us to an abandoned church near that slow turn, surrounded by woods and fields. It was where our ancestors would have come to pray, she said, and a number of Roses lay beneath worn stone markers in the graveyard. Rev. Rose's father, however, didn't seem to be among them. Yet another picturesque dead end.

On the way back to the castle, Ms. Foster explained that in Scotland, the first son inherited the chief's title and land. "When the chief could afford to give the second and third son some property," she said, "he would." She pointed out a grand estate peeking above a line of pine trees: Holme Rose, property the eighth Baron of Kilravock gave his second son, Alexander, in the 1400s.

We toured nearby Nairn, a fishing port ruled for centuries by the Roses, then drove through fields to the Bronze-Age Clava Cairns, two bus-size circles of stones set within an eerily silent grove. As we explored, Ms. Foster asked.

"Remember how we couldn't get any further than Lewis Rose's father?"

An older edition of the Church of Scotland book contained an interesting footnote, she said, pointing to the entry for the reverend: "Lewis Rose, grandson of David Rose of Leanach, descended of Holme Rose."

Ten minutes later, our car crunched onto the tree-lined drive leading to Holme Rose, the stone manor we had spied beyond the trees. Waiting for us was John Rose-Miller, an older gentleman who had been born there—and who was our cousin, many times removed.

Dad and I were both right, it turns out. We are connected to the chiefs of Kilravock, but the link is a tenuous one. It goes back more than 500 years, when one of our forebears founded the Holme Rose line.

On the way back to Edinburgh, my father and I decided that we were not disappointed by what we'd learned. If anything, we were happy to adopt the Holme Rose family motto. " 'I Dare' is far more interesting than 'Constant and True,' " Dad said. And I agreed. (Story ends)

Gisela's news story received plenty of attention in our immediate family because her mother and brother, unlike me, did not know all the intricate details of that amazing Scottish historical trip.

Years before the horrifying Kilravock Inn fire event, Julie and John purchased the Kilravock from Julie's two brothers and sister, my Mom, to start a part time inn in the summer, and in the fall, winter and spring, to house the girl students attending the co-educational Forman School on Norfolk Road north of the town.

Years later, when Kilravock had long become a year around inn, Julie used to park her car below at the inn and walk up a small hill through a pine forest to the log cabin.

The cabin was built in the late 1960s as part of the inn accommodations. Years later, it became home to my wife, Ina, and myself, and eventually our two children, Gisela and Tommie. Julie had loaned Ina and I the cabin after she had allowed us to stay at the inn in an extra room on the second floor soon after our marriage in 1970. We needed a home.

When Julie was young, she used to play a musical instrument and studied to be an opera singer in Paris, France. As a result, she had the most wondrous melodic consciousness, compelling her to hum and sing to herself. Gorgeous sounding vocal melodies became part of her spirit.

Every time Julie visited us, while walking uphill on that dirt lane lined with tall pines, she would whistle and hum sweet tunes. Often I could also hear the calls of Cardinals: booowee, bowee boop or cheer, cheer, cheer chip, chip, chip chip chip.

By sight, not song, we knew they were Cardinals when we spotted the sharp red colored male with his triangular head hat flying from branch to branch. The female Cardinal is a gorgeous gray color with red streaks on its wings and tufted triangular head, and could be seen only occasionally in the thick pines. But we could hear them both singing frequently.

To this day, my memories of Cardinals chirping loudly as Julie whistled or hummed her charming tunes, while they both moved through the pines, are intertwined. As a result, cardinals, those gorgeous flying, singing feathered creatures, are my all-time favorite bird.

I have nourished them and other feathered friends with bird feeders since I was a child. But cardinals and their songs became part of my soul because I will always remember those wild tunes accompanying Julie's pine forest humming and light, charming whistling.

Here are two Cardinal lovers!

How do I remember Uncle John? I still can see his handsome, loving face, hear his calm low voice and remember his spiritual faith and related moral advice. He was very athletic and taught me and other students to play hockey on a pond below the school.

His qualities eventually helped me survive difficulties with tough experiences as an army lieutenant and as an investigative reporter.

After my Forman School experiences, Dad wanted me to move on before college to the Choate School in Wallingford, Connecticut, for two years where he had spent a graduation year before going on to Yale University for a Bachelor of Arts degree.

My biggest joy at Choate was becoming a two-year varsity soccer player, a sport inspiring me to play on for another varsity team when I graduated and then entered Middlebury College in Vermont. I mention this because one of the most inspiring experiences I ever had was playing soccer in college for coach Joe Morrone.

Joe was not only a wondrous leader and coach, but a compelling and charismatic personality, influencing his players not only to stay in top physical shape, but to become the best possible athletes and thoughtful, moral competitors that they could possibly be. He worked us to the bone in practices. Sometimes, Joe ran laps around and around the field with us to stay in shape. Then, during competitions, he patrolled the sidelines, holding a soccer clip board he filled with notes, sometimes crashing it to the ground during the game's emotional moments.

After leaving Middlebury years later, Joe became nationally renowned as the University of Connecticut's soccer coach. Eventually working 27 years for that team, he was inducted into the National Soccer Coaches Association of America Hall of Fame in 2002. The UCONN soccer stadium is named after him, for good reason.

Here is a quote in The New York Times: "Coach Morrone laid the blueprint not only for soccer at UConn but as importantly for college soccer in the entire country," the 2015 UConn coach Ray Reid said, adding that Morrone, who had recently passed away, was one of the first soccer coaches to actively recruit players.

Many years after I had graduated from Middlebury in 1962, I missed Joe so dearly that I decided to drive a couple of hours down from my Litchfield, Connecticut home to New Brunswick, New Jersey, where Rutgers University was hosting a national soccer tourney involving UCONN.

I arrived just minutes before UCONN's team rushed on the field for its game. I walked up to the top row of the aluminum stands and spotted Joe next to the team's bench intensively conferring with a player. Without hesitation, I yelled out, "Hey Joe, how the heck are you?!" Within seconds, Joe turned, without even spotting me, and exclaimed: "Dennie, get down here to play fullback!" I thought, how could he recognize my voice after not seeing me for years?

But, years after that day, in 2015, I experienced one of the saddest days of my life! While inside the historic 1700s salt box home of ours, I received a telephone call from Bob Hall, a captain of the Middlebury soccer team before I was. I hadn't talked to Bob, I think, since we played on his organized hockey team together many years after our college soccer days.

He immediately gave me the sad news: Joe Morrone was very close to death, and I needed to telephone him right away. I immediately dialed Joe's number repeatedly, but it was busy - obviously with calls from the scores of those who knew him.

Finally, I was so relieved to ring in and hear his voice. It sounded so wonderful, that friendly Morrone tone! We must have talked about past soccer playing and our experiences together and apart for 30 to 40 minutes before we said "Good-Bye!" There had not been one mention of his terminal health condition. When the connection ended, I began to weep and could not stop for several minutes.

Here's a picture of Joe below, shown at a game by the Associated Press.

I was fortunate to experience many wondrous and emotional relationships in my life.

I met my wife Ina while on vacation from my newspaper job in the summer of 1969 on Elbow Beach in Bermuda, the same month when the first U.S. astronaut reached the moon. She was visiting the island on a sabbatical from teaching school kids in Flensburg, Germany.

Ina was living with her close cousins, the Lewins, whose four children years later eventually became close friends with our own children, Gisela and Tommie.

Our initial chanceful meeting on a beautiful Elbow Beach was an amazing and eventually joy-full experience. I spotted the gorgeous woman on a sunny day with her cousin, Gaby Lewin, and her two young children, Megan and Andreas, roving the beach.

As a bachelor, I was trying to figure out which of the young ladies was the Mom and who was single. I came to the conclusion that it was Ina after she stayed on for a while in the late afternoon, when all the others in that group had left the beach.

A day or so later, I saw Ina again. This time she was alone on the beach, and I observed her swim out with a blond Labrador called Bwanna. I soon jumped in after them and followed them far out over the ocean to see if I could get to know her somehow. Since Ina is and was a better swimmer than I, I was not used to swimming out that far. It was then, far from shore, that I dared to get close enough to exclaim: "That dog must be an Olympic swimmer!"

Ina slowed, looked back at me quizzically, said absolutely NOTHING, looked away, and continued her swim! I swam back to shore as a wounded eligible bachelor.

But sometime later (I think that very day), after a crew of guys stopped showing off by playing with a soccer ball right around Ina's prone body in the sand, and ultimately left the beach, I got the guts to approach her and start a conversation.

At the end of it, I asked her where she was going that evening, thinking I would ask her out on a date. However, Ina quickly told me she was going to dinner at the Hog Penny Pub with her cousins. So I replied, quite swiftly for me, "Oh, see you there probably, because I'm going for a drink!"

That very evening Gaby and Nicky, her husband, arrived with Ina while I was sitting and drinking at the bar. The three of them continued on into the restaurant area.

I quickly walked down and away from the bar into the restaurant, moved boldly right up to their table, strode eye-to-eye with Ina and greeted her. She looked up as if she had never, ever seen me before!

Extremely embarrassed, I started walking away. But, immediately, Nicky caught my attention by exclaiming, "SIT DOWN!" I was so startled, that I did exactly what he said. I then explained that I arrived at their table simply to see Ina again, after we had met earlier and talked on the beach. Ina, fortunately, now recognized me.

After we all conversed for a while, Nicky and Gaby invited me to a movie they were planning on going to with Ina, starring Ronald Reagan.

That was my first extended time ever with Ina, and it turned out not to be my last. Somehow, I later met up with her and convinced her to visit me somewhere in the USA, because she informed me she was planning a post Bermudian trip to North Carolina. We did indeed arrange to meet up, after Ina's Carolina excursion, I believe in New York City, so our relationship miraculously continued.

Months later, of course, after phone calls and letters back and forth from Germany and the U.S.A., I proposed to Ina after we were coming back from Vermont skiing, and she accepted. Then, we got married joyfully in Germany. Here we are below then.

A year after our wedding, Ina gave birth, first to Gisela, and then three years later, to Tommie. The two of them, now adults, are now married and have spouses of their own: Carsten and Amely. Now Gisela and Carsten have three young children, two girls, Cosima and Paloma and a boy, Cassian, while Tommie and Amely, have young girl, Patience.

All of those adults have fascinating careers. Carsten works as a supervisor in a business involving solar panels, carbon fiber, and thermal processing equipment, while Gisela is a freelance travel and style writer. Tommie has a sports clothing and hat business, Dedicate. In the meantime, Amely Greeven has written health and lifestyle books with well-known personalities for Harper Collins and Rodale and for brands such as NYC's Juice Generation.

CHAPTER 3

MILITARY INVESTIGATIVE EXPERIENCES HELP INSPIRE A CAREER IN NEWS REPORTING

As a young man I despised even the thought of the military. Dad and Mom, as well as Aunt Julie and Uncle John, were always advocates for world peace. At Middlebury College, I even flunked out of the ROTC course that would have effortlessly made me what I eventually became: an Army second lieutenant. Amazingly, though, some years after leaving the military for good, I became very thankful for being drafted into the Army, despite my reluctance to serve.

After graduating from Middlebury with a Bachelor of Arts degree as an American Literature major, I worked for some months as a college admissions interviewer for prospective students. In 1963, after leaving that job, which prepared me in many ways for news reporting interviewing, my mandatory draft into the Army arrived. I faced an initial eight and a half weeks of basic training at Ft. Dix, New Jersey.

I thought those weeks were largely tedious: crawling along the ground with an M-16 rifle, cleaning toilets and marching from place to place in formation. But, as I wrote my parents, there were also helpful courses in military justice, land navigation and first aid. I even told them: "Despite the many drawbacks of Army life, I am gaining much valuable experience for anything I decide to do later on."

However, to avoid the more annoying basics, I applied to become a driver for a huge Army hauling truck, but failed the truck's more intricate driving skills test. It was very disappointing to return to irritating day-to-day orders. Once I graduated from basic training, I feared more boredom as a basic private, so I applied for and was accepted in Artillery Officer Candidate School at Ft. Sill, Oklahoma.

The school's three-step mandatory advancement there consisted of three student classes: lower, middle and upper. Lower classmen were intensively ordered around and harassed by middle and upper classmen, as well as actual Army officers. But middle and upper classes faced their own brand of discouraging indignities as well.

It was, discouragingly, some four months before graduation as a second lieutenant. It seemed to take years. The daily pressurized training crippled everyone's spirits.

Lower classmen were awakened around 5 a.m. by screaming military trainers, standing feet away. We jumped into shorts, an undershirt and sneakers. Then, we were immediately forced to run the roads for miles in formation. Once back, sweating, we changed into our standard Army khaki work outfits. After sitting straight up at bodily attention, while being watched, over a meager breakfast, we were harangued from maintenance job after job, like raking soil on the run around barracks after barracks.

Off and on we were marched by officers to a field with M-16 rifles over our shoulders. There we took the officers' instructive orders. While standing at attention, we gradually learned how to smoothly move the weapon from holding it parallel to our bodies on the ground to our shoulders.

After a few weeks, I couldn't take the harassment anymore, so dejectedly, I quit the school. I was immediately ashamed of myself for dropping out. Astonishingly, after a short break of a few days on my own, during which I saw the Oklahoma Sooners play football one Saturday, I volunteered to reenter lower class officer training. Why?! I felt deeply depressed about my failure to endure training. But, I was the only reentry for those who, like me, had quit school early.

As a returnee, I immediately wondered why my former classmates, now middle classmen, reduced their harassment of me, once again a lower class man! Well, they, from their own very recent experience, fully understood what I was suffering again, and couldn't believe I had returned.

I don't remember exactly when it was, but at some point, we were forced into a bus to actually act upon our artillery training with the 105 mm Howitzer M3, sitting outside. We were rushed out on a gigantic never-ending field where a number of Howitzers were lined up parallel and all pointed in one direction, each set to fire at separate targets.

We were not to fire at these weapons, but to determine with observation how far or near its target was and then give abrupt and distinct orders to the gunner as to the coordinates so he could adjust the weapon on the target. If the weapon's-shell explosion missed, we needed to readjust target instructions. As I recall with some fear, my instructions sent the first round right beyond the required actual target area. The supervising officer screamed to adjust fire. I did closer to target. But, that's all I can remember.

Then, a day or two later, it was the more familiar weapon's instructions. It was that boring M-16 rifle repetitious body-movement training from the ground, holding alongside the right leg, then up to the shoulder.

Once after being hypnotized into this repetition, we were all immediately halted in mid-rifle handling and marched back into our barracks for a rare, long break. We soon learned from a loudspeaker that the abrupt end to our training was caused by horrifying historic news. President John F. Kennedy had been assassinated just hours before that very mid-day, Friday, November 22, 1963, while in a motorcade through Dealey Plaza in downtown Dallas, Texas.

We never had time in school to truly contemplate or read about that national tragedy. Amazingly, despite all the ongoing torment, I graduated through all three classes. My weight had dropped from approximately 190 pounds to about 160.

Part of that reduction came from all the disciplinary 25 to 50 push-ups and the even harsher penalties of jogging up the school's MB-4 Mountain, a four-mile round trip. Once, I was such a bad boy that I had to do two in succession. Another time, one of the officers, pressing us up hill in his shorts and T-shirt, fainted to the ground. I could hear candidates, in full, hot uniforms, muffled chuckling alongside me.

Now that I look back, it is for sure that this daily intimidation training matured me as a mentally stronger person, allowing me to recover from errors without, as they say, throwing in the towel.

Later, as a fresh, new second lieutenant, I immediately decided to get out of the artillery division. I never was one who liked to fire any kind of a weapon. So I applied instead to become an Army Intelligence officer. That turned out to be a fascinating three months training in Baltimore, Maryland, as opposed to those previous frightening Ft. Sill experiences.

This educational training unexpectedly turned out to be training for my work years later as an investigative reporter and may have even subconsciously lured me into those later detailed news inquiries.

The school had two absolutely incredibly fun courses. One was a foot surveillance of either spies or intelligence violators. The other involved interrogating talented and convincing actors and actresses appearing on stage and playing the parts of possible security violators or troublesome security job applicants.

The surveillance was carried out within the crowded City of Baltimore with quite a few separate targets, called rabbits, each followed by three student investigative agents.

In order to stay in disguise, the agents were broken up to surveil their rabbits: one discretely behind the prey and two following one another at a distance on the opposite side of the street. Those two, one at a time, alternatively and occasionally replaced their mate across the street to hopefully assure their target did not discover he was being followed.

At one point, the rabbits, having conspired to do this previously, all met inside a diminutive coffee shop. Those rabbits must have been laughing into their drinks. Looking through the shop's windows outside on the streets, their investigative agents having to avoid bumping into one another while surreptitiously moving around the street blocks.

That other fascinating course, involving student interrogations of actors, who were playing alleged spies or security violators, created some real amusement for the student audience as well. Each interrogator was selected for his interview without any warning. He then walked out of the classroom and knocked on a hallway door to await his quiz target's answer.

The actor or actress led him to a stage, inside which was a one-way glass sight wall allowing only the other students to become spectators from the neighboring room. Laughter erupted frequently from the observers when a spy actor or actress decided to softly mess up their inquisitors. This could not have been better training for any news reporter, including an investigative one.

After basic training, a harsh artillery officer candidate school and intelligence training, I was initially stationed in Paju Ri, South Korea, and a year later sent to Washington, D.C. Indeed, that intelligence corps service work, after I left the Army, was to become my primary inspiration behind my gradual move from routine news reporting work to more complex investigations of political and corporate corruption.

The North Koran spies I investigated with other agents, with the help of Korean interpreters who worked with us in the small 191st Military Intelligence Detachment, were incredibly fascinating. I still remember one riveting interview I had with a North Korean spy through wondrous interpreter Yu Taek Chin. Inside a cramped interrogation room, Yusi became so dominant with the cross examination that I had to constantly interrupt him to squeeze my own queries in. Now, I think, 'Too bad I couldn't have written news stories about those fascinating 'day to day experiences!'

In fact, one of those escapades did hit the newspapers. It was a North Korean mini submarine entering the DMZ through the Han River Estuary.

My fellow lieutenant, Bruce Bailey, who too, coincidentally graduated from Middlebury College a year after me, ended up assigned to that very same diminutive intelligence unit. Here we are (below) standing together inside our unit in Paju-Ri.

I am alone standing on the submarine in the top photo below, while Bruce and I are pictured both standing on the craft in the bottom two photos below.

Unfortunately, the North Korean occupants had fled before we, or any soldiers, could find, capture and interrogate them. Here's the story in an area newspaper:

MIDGET SUB FOUND IN HAN RIVER

Stars And Stripes Korea Bureau Thursday July 8, 1965

SEOUL – An old Japanese two-man midget submarine, apparently used by North Koreans, was discovered Monday stuck on a mud flat and abandoned in the Han River estuary,

The sub was spotted at low tide by a reconnaissance patrol of the 19th Republic of Korea army regiment Combat Team about a mile from where the Han and Imjin Rivers join. First to board the sub was 1st Lt. Bruce V. Bailey of the 191st Military Intelligence Detachment who found several items identifiable with the North Korean military.

Among items Bruce discovered were grenades, clips of ammunition, food and a tank filled with diesel fuel.

US Navy officials in Korea said the sub is 15 feet long, six feet high and weighs approximately two tons. Officials said Wednesday it had not been determined how long the craft had been stuck in the mud or what its mission was when it was abandoned.

US Army men said the sub, which bore no markings, was crudely constructed and probably of World War II vintage because similar types of Japanese submarines used at Pearl Harbor in 1941 were of much better quality.

The news story ended by describing the military removal of the sub from the river as the joint US-Korean investigation continued discovering suspicions that espionage was indeed involved.

Unfortunately, the North Korean occupants had fled before we, or any soldiers, could find, capture and interrogate them.

Only three weeks later, the United Nations Command reported in the very same newspaper that the sub, named the Kim Il Sung, was indeed a spying venture. Kim Il Sung, says Wikipedia, "was the supreme leader of North Korea from its establishment in 1948 until his death in 1994. He held the posts of Prime Minister from 1948 to 1972 and President from 1972 to 1994."

However, North Korean officials called these submarine spying charges "vile propaganda and vicious personals attacks" on their leader. But, on the very day this submarine was discovered sunk, the United Nations reported that during fierce opposing gunfire, two North Korean spies were captured by Korean policemen who lost two of their own in the battle.

The two prisoners reportedly confessed they were sent into South Korea "to commit sabotage and kidnapping." Two other spies were reported to have escaped. But it was not clear from the news stories whether these four spies were connected to the submarine. And our intelligence unit was not assigned search for the spies along with the Korean military and police. Our mission was usually to take part in spy interrogations after spies were captured by the police or the military.

Secret intelligence missions were fascinating experiences, but sometimes not as fun as entertaining time off with our interrogating Korean partners. Charlie O, a serious, experienced interpreter-investigator, never let his job get in the way of his fun wild creature hunting adventures.

Despite the fact that he knew I was never a hunter, he invited me out one morning for a serious cross-country hunting experience. I was a bit reluctant considering my love of wild creatures and my hunting inexperience, but I was to be ashamed of myself had I refused Charlie O, a close colleague whom I trusted would be a thoughtful, not a cruel, hunter.

HERE IS CHARLIE O, A GREAT GUY AND INTERPRETER HANGING OUT WITH ME INSIDE THE 191ST MITITARY INTELLIGENCE DETACHMENT

One morning we drove the Jeep into the 25th Republic of Korea sector adjacent to the border with North Korea. We left the 191st Military Detachment in Paju ri and arrived at our destination about an hour later. Before doing the trip, we had to coordinate with our Korean Army counterparts. They got us a counterintelligence corps guide and a well-managed Korean hunter with his dog.

I was at first impressed about how much they worried about our safety until I later learned there were a lot of old landmines in the area which could have detonated had we stepped on them. Fortunately, Charlie brought an old hunting associate with him who had 'scoured' this area numerous times.

We started out quickly because the hunting dog soon flushed out three pheasants from a riverbed. I didn't have the opportunity to shoot my shotgun because the Koreans were quick to fire and missed.

We began moving rather quickly as the Koreans' thirst for game increased after they missed their initial targets. As we were just about to leave an area of our initial focus, we noticed that the "papason's" dog was circulating in on a live object of interest near a thicket. We waited there a while, and then started to sweep the area ourselves for game.

As I was walking directly forward, a pheasant came up almost directly under me. He was so fast and I was so inexperienced that it was gone before I could even raise my weapon. Charlie O and the others spotted it as its silhouette hit the sky.

Three hunters shot and missed, but Charlie O, with his keen sense of timing, brought it down. The old mongrel dog, a rather shaggy animal, immediately hustled to the spot of the landing and waited until his papasan boss could get there.

I requested a look at the bird and when the papa a brought it to me, it was still alive. Charlie had merely shot it in the wing. Before I had my basic instinct to call the National Parks Conservation Association, Charlie strolled over, took it from my hands and broke its neck over his gun barrel. Then, he strapped the very same neck under the back of the papasan's belt. This was certainly a quick initiation for me into Korean hunting.

Shortly thereafter, we embarked on one of the longest and leg tiring sweeps of any countryside that I, in my relatively short life, have ever undertaken. We climbed upward along long rice paddy valleys, climbed little side valleys indented in the mountains and made our way through marshy areas, fighting against hordes of long straw-colored marsh weeds. Such a furious initiation was driving me into the ground, so I slowed down a bit as my companions disappeared.

Before I knew it, I was hearing many gun shots coming from up in a valley. I moved swiftly from my position on the hill to attempt to get a better look at what was going on, but trees and big shrubs blocked my view. All of a sudden, I spotted a deer running full speed down the valley toward me and jumping one rice paddy to another on a lower level. I was slow to respond, but as the deer was running on a diagonal in my direction, I started to run down the mountain to cut it off. And here it is below.

I ran into all sorts of natural plant and rock barriers on the way down and thus could not concentrate on siting the deer. By the time I had made it down to the bottom of the slopes, my legs had been whipped by sharp weeds, my breath was waging a war on my lungs and the deer was 'jinagan, obso' or gone. Still, today, I remember the stinging of my legs and my shortness of breath so vividly that I can see and feel them and picture the scene

This wild one's escape from my shotgun, as well as the pheasant's earlier, freshened my appetite for the hunt. I quickly joined my fellow hunters who, by this time, had bagged themselves a total of four or five pheasants. They had already finished sweeping one side of the valley and were starting on the other when I joined them.

While making up our way up one of the many up one of the many mountain indent valley lets, the energetic hunting canine began his frequent excited smelling, rushing and circling. The papasan knew right away that Bess, as he called her with respect, was just about to flush a bird.

We all stopped and waited expectantly with our weapons poised at the ready. I heard a flapping of wings about 50 yards away and in a flash spotted an airborne pheasant. I pointed my shotgun and pulled light on the trigger. The bird dropped to the ground, but not before I had heard a simultaneous gun shot from the papasan's weapon. I couldn't really tell whose shot had hit the bird.

However, before I could say a word, the papasan was loudly saying, ''Number one shot. Your number one shot.'' So what could I do with doubt hanging, but hesitantly accept his aggressive praise. Charlie soon came over with the dead pheasant in hand and strapped it to the back of my pants.

From then on, I knew I had been initiated into the club, the club of those who know the feeling of a successful hunt, even if it is only one well aimed shot. They knew I was a rookie who needed to be baptized in the hunt. One could easily imagine how I was swaggered and strode through the fields and bushes instead of walking to and fro like one with no experience. My energy increased to the point that my stiff moving legs knew no barrier to a path too long or too steep.

Shortly thereafter, we finished the hunt and went back to count our kill and eat the Army rations that Charlie and I had brought with us. Once we had been collected in the group, we noticed that Charlie's friend, Yi, was missing from the gathering.

Then, while we were still talking and eating, we heard a succession of gun shots. About a half hour later, there were another series of shot gun blasts, while our talking and eating were still underway. Then, Mr. Yi came into camp with a badger in hand, hanging by its hind feet. Yi's shotgun was slung casually across his free arm. And, two pheasants were strapped to his belt.

We congratulated him, looked over his badger and went back to our seats to finish the luncheon. That afternoon we all continued the sweeps of the morning in other areas of the mountain country. There was little success, including my missed shot at another pheasant. Then Mr. Yi spotted deer while on the other side of the hill from me.

He fired three shots, and by the time the last one was fired, I had joined him.

The deer was in its death throws in the long, wild grass. Bess, the papasan's dog, smelled the fresh blood and leaped in for the kill, but the old man called him off with fierce orders and reprimands.

Minutes later, after all had closely observed the deer, Mr. Yi carried it back to the road and covered it with weeds in temporary storage so that he could continue his overly intense hunt.

On the sweeps that followed my companions bagged a few more pheasants, however, that was a heavy anti-climax to Mr. Yi's intensive hunting efforts earlier. The momentum of the chase had finally slowed and the papasan insisted we had hunted out the area. So, we all threw our weapons over our shoulders and ended the chase.

That night Charlie O, Mr. Yi, Captain Kim who arranged the hunt, and assorted others had a celebration of our afternoon adventures in a ginseng house, a restaurant. Meanwhile, outside, the people of the village all crowded around our parked jeep in amazement, so once in a while one of us had to leave the party and check to see that no one ''slicked'' our game.

Soon afterward, I wrote my parents and said I hoped Mom was not alarmed by my initiation as a hunter.

I cannot remember further details of this escapade decades later, but it is hard to believe that I was not beginning to feel saddened and ashamed by all these wild bird and animal killings.

A later experience with my son showed hypocrisy on my part with my Korean hunting and shooting at squirrels

I will confess that I used to get raving mad at squirrels and bears invading bird feeders I have lovingly managed since I was a young boy. In fact, I, as a father of my own young boy, used to throw rocks and fire BB guns at squirrels who were jumping on my feeders. But at one point, that youngster made me into a squirrel sympathizer.

I was walking outside the house when I spotted a weird shelf feeder attached low to a big pine tree and was shocked. I turned back to look at the house and there in the door's big window was my son Tommie, as a young boy, smiling.

I rushed over, opened the door and maddeningly wanted to know what he was smiling about. Immediately, he exclaimed that I was a "dummy" to constantly be attacking squirrels and possibly hurting them. I fell silent. Later, I thought about his critique, decided he was absolutely right and never physically attacked squirrels again. Now I just scream at them. But I didn't learn that particular lesson until many years after leaving the Army, becoming a news reporter, getting married and raising two children.

These days the closest I get to hunting is chasing after black bears who attack my bird feeders. As far as that's concerned, one incident with a black bear is worth mentioning. That particular bear crushed my metal feeder to the ground and lay down to eat bird seed. I spotted him and rushed out of the house toward the beast and screamed! The bear quickly got up and ran away toward the nearby brook with me after him.

Suddenly, that big bear stopped for a second looked back at me and instead of continuing toward the brook, ran parallel to me toward a second bird feeder, hanging high over his head from the branch of a huge maple tree. He then stopped at the tree base, stood up, leaned his paw on the tree and stared at me. I could not believe that bear's total change of mind so completely that I started laughing. Fortunately, that bear changed his mind, did not climb and instead again ran away toward the brook.

I never remember participating in wild animal chasing or hunting as I had in Korea at any time afterwards. Thank goodness, because looking back, my increased love of wild creatures, leading to authoring a nature short story book, makes me feel guilty about my part in that Korean hunting excursion.

It does not, however, change my powerful respect for Charlie O, the enthusiastic hunter, who was an intelligent and brave military companion. Investigative Army Intelligence experiences with him sparked great admiration for his culture and country. I am still constantly ashamed of myself for never returning to Korea to reawaken memories and especially to visit with those wondrous Korean interpreters.

Here some of them below with ''Yousi'' or Yu Taek Chin, far left above, Charlie O, far right above, ''Doc'' Yi, middle lower and Kimsi, right lower. I am ashamed I cannot remember the wonderful guy sitting in the far left front. The two men in the middle above were not in the unit when I was there.

After that approximately year-long Korean assignment, and before retiring from the Army and moving on to The Courant, I toiled in the nation's capital as a plain clothes military investigator, checking on alleged and involved security violations by civilians or Army service members.

This experience was extremely valuable. Not only did it influence my choice to go into the news business, but it, just like prior military intelligence experiences, eventually, within a couple of years, induced me into investigative reporting for the rest of my news working life. Sometimes the fact digging can be scary!

CHAPTER 4

THE DANGERS AND CHALLENGES OF INVESTIGATIVE REPORTING

During my career, while writing about Organized Crime activities, I was fortunate to have been threatened only a handful of times from alleged professional criminals. Luckily they happened over telephone conversations with threatening trash haulers, and not person to person on the street.

The Nest, advising couples on comfortable lifestyles, says: "Good investigative reporters must possess a strong sense of right and wrong. Their sound ethics and finely-tuned moral compass guide them in battling to stomp out crime and corruption. Investigative reporters call upon these faculties to complete
sometimes dangerous and exhausting tasks, including meeting secretly with known criminals, scanning financial reports for hours and interviewing dozens of individuals to corroborate a source's allegations.

Good investigative journalists must believe it is their responsibility and civic obligation to uncover facts to ensure fairness, accuracy and transparency."

I worked with at least one other reporter from another newspaper who regularly dug out mob created government irregularities, but never discussed with me the obvious threats that must have been made to him. As a reporter within the same chain of newspapers, I was fortunate to work in the 1980s for over a year with Long Island Newsday's amazing investigative team leader, Bob Greene.

Bob helped create Investigative Reporters and Editors, IRE, in 1975, the year before Dan Bolles, a reporter for The Arizona Republic was murdered. At that time, Bolles was in the midst of exposing corruption and organized crime in Arizona.

Opening his car on June 2, 1976, Bolles got in, started the engine and it exploded with an incredible blast! Bolles' eventual death from that car bomb led to an arrest of the slayer due in part to a vague identification by fatally wounded Bolles. Soon afterwards on his hospital bed, he identified that same suspect in a photo shown him by police. Those investigators found that very name in Bolles' typewriter soon afterward.

Bolles died just days before an IRE Conference.

In the aftermath of the slaying, Green and other IRS members became convinced that what Bolles was probing was not getting unearthed. So Bob gathered a group of IRE reporters together from various newspapers country-wide, and convinced their bosses to allow them to investigate those very corrupt activities

They spent six months roaming Phoenix and its vicinity while putting together a 23-part series that expanded the scope of the investigation Bolles had begun. It ran in newspapers across the country.

Our totally unrelated Courant-Newsday probe all started eight years later. That was inspired when Theodore Ted Driscoll, The Courant's first full time modern investigative reporter, and I met up with Greene at a 1984 Investigative Reporters and Editors conference in Miami, Florida. Ironically, The Courant and Newsday were to become part of the same Chicago Tribune newspaper chain a year more than a decade and a half later.

Greene, who had, the year we met, been recently investigating Mafia activities in the construction industry. He encouraged us to look into a contractor in Connecticut which was allegedly working along with a Long Island contractor to dominate sales of supplies of road building trap rock.

On July 25, 1984, not long after our initial IRE conference meeting, Bob Greene and Joseph Demma, Bob's Newsday investigative colleague, came to Bridgeport to lecture myself, Driscoll and two other Courant colleagues about alleged corruption among large road contractors, unions and organized crime.

The corrupt activity on Long Island involved contractors paying off unions to avoid costly road building strikes, while the unions themselves were being manipulated by organized criminals. Greene and Demma then described how certain road builders dominated the industry and created monopolies, attracting investigations by federal authorities in New York.

The session lasted for about three hours and 20 minutes and became one of the most informative and inspiring briefings in my then 18 years working as a journalist! The major focus of the discussions was corrupt activities within the road building industry.

From his very own experiences, Greene, who ultimately led his newspaper, Newsday, to two Pulitzer Prizes, detailed some of the constant corrupt habits in the road building construction industry. As a result of that very corruption, said Greene, a number of road builders in both states are dominating the industry, creating a monopolies and inducing federal investigations in New York and Connecticut areas.

Here is a smiling Bob Greene, in news tribute below on the next page.

From http://www.thomasmaierbooks.com/2008/06/tribute-to-robert-w-greene-bob-greene.html

Typically, he said, unions must be paid off by contractors to avoid costly road building strikes; and because some construction unions have been controlled by organized crime, it is improbable that many contractors can remain clean.

Greene suggested that if we started our own joint probe of this industry, we could create momentum for many hard hitting, in-depth stories for both newspapers. He totally convinced us of the merits this rare joint newspaper investigation.

As a result, we, with two teams of reporters, began digging out widespread questionable activities within several related and cooperating companies in the road building industry in Connecticut and New York. In doing so, The Courant and Newsday were collaborating in a specific plan to simultaneously publish our own versions of the construction industry stories in both newspapers.

Unfortunately, after many months of work, The Courant's detailed story was eliminated with certain trepidation by the then publisher, Michael Davies, while Newsday's investigation continued.

But, before that story's killing happened, I told Davies I would keep the story alive by convincing the previously reluctant target company executive to be interviewed, even though he had refused repeatedly to cooperate earlier. I received assistance from Courant Reporter Gerry Demeusy who had written a small positive book about the company. He contacted the construction executive and convinced him to talk to me.

Indeed, that powerful construction company head surprisingly allowed me a visit to his contracting company office and politely showed me around the facility. But ultimately, back in his plush office, he refused to answer any of my specific queries regarding what The Courant's lengthy probe discovered about his firm's questionable operations.

As a result, Editor Davies continued his story rejection. The killing of that story was the most disappointing episode I ever experienced as a journalist. Even today many of the details of that hard and dangerous reporting work are etched in my mind.

Afterward, Jon Lender, an investigative colleague, not involved in the story's effort, asked me to look out into The Courant's large parking lot to humorously exclaim: 'See that big light pole out there? Underneath it is where the editor buried your story.'

Indeed, I was asked later by a doctor-psychologist what one of my greatest life disappointments had been, and I reawakened this crushed investigative story in full detail.

My respect for Bob Greene's amazing leadership and courage to finally convince his own editors to publish their accounts of those fascinating road contracting industry irregularities will never leave me. In fact, during Bob's own initial failure to convince an editor of certain story plans, he said he became frustrated enough to crash his fist against a wall that separated the two of them.

Today most problematic nationwide, as investigative reporting weakens, is the disheartening of sophisticated news readers who care deeply about what is really happening outside their own routine daily news readings. And some of these readers may even be honest and caring government investigators who are induced by an investigative news story to conduct their own in depth probes.

As suggested, most negatively constraining to the public interest is this loss of in-depth newspaper corruption probes of hidden criminal, immoral or questionable activity.

Think about it! It was The Washington Post's experienced investigative reporters, Carl Bernstein and Bob Woodward who were called in to work on the huge Watergate Scandal in the summer of 1972. And, in part due to their amazing probes, the wide-ranging political scandal concluded with the resignation of President Richard Nixon two years later.

CHAPTER 5

DEVELOPMENTS HARMING INVESTIGATIVE REPORTERS

The crucial and cornerstone example of Watergate and its investigation began fading out nationwide close to two decades ago. Eventually, our employer, The Hartford Courant, the nation's oldest newspaper in continuous circulation since October 1764, began cutting back on its own in-depth and investigative news in the late 1990s and early 2000s.

Year after year, it started and continued laying off experienced reporters, capable of in-depth reporting.

Here is what I wrote for Truthout.org to describe that news culture after I began my freelance writing career in 2005, when I retired from The Courant.

"If some doomsday industry analysts are to be believed, newspapers are laid out and stacked neatly inside their own future death warehouses, not only in the United States, but worldwide."

"As newspaper size shrinks, experienced reporters and editors are replaced by relative greenhorns. Then, the comparative evidence in daily published reporting shows a wide variety of in-depth stories and features morphing into larger sensational headlines, bigger photos, news graphics and repetitive bad news dominated by politics, crime and war."

Nieman Reports, which follows the news industry closely, said the following development might have been an in-depth news cut back cause inside scores of newspapers. It reports:

"Data suggest that the erosion in newspaper advertising and audience during the 1990's was at least exacerbated, in part, by the business strategies put in place at newspapers to emphasize profit over market share," says Nieman Reports.

This very opinion evolved from Nieman defining its mission as "a dynamic set of initiatives to promote and elevate the standards of journalism and educate and support those poised to make important contributions to its future."

Those initiatives are getting much weaker today, according to knowledgeable experts in the news business. In just the next eleven years, "newspapers in their current form will become insignificant" in this country, while other countries worldwide will come later", Future Exploration Network said in 2014, according to ACI Information Group.

See https://aci.info/2014/08/29/when-will-newspapers-become-extinct/

During the early 2000s, not long after the news decline time frame mentioned by Nieman, The Courant's editors gradually began to shift myself and other experienced reporters into mostly daily news work, instead of comprehensive research, taking weeks or months to explore. The paper does still have investigative reporters but not the emphasis on such work as there used to be.

When I was there the editors increasingly forestalled me from utilizing the time, research and intensive desire to eventually uncover overlooked criminality and immorality among office holders, entrepreneurs, as well as freelance law and rule breakers. The paper still works on such inquiries, but far less than it used to do in the 1970s, 1980s and 1990s.

Fighting Intimidation

It was in 2001, after being an investigator on and off for three decades, that I was suddenly transferred to more elementary local court coverage in New Britain. As a rookie reporter, decades earlier, I had been assigned to such basic town coverage. That was before I began creating some occasional investigative exposes and then becoming a police, and next, a court reporter.

If I managed to uncover corrupt activities, editors usually allowed me to drop normal daily assignments and move into those longer-range inquiries. Even later, for a while, I specialized solely in investigative reporting, sometimes with wondrous reporting partners.

But once I was transferred to New Britain from Hartford, I was not given the time I had in the past for such reporting. Instead, I was assigned to daily coverage of that local New Britain Superior Court. Again, that news work typically was given to the less veteran and experienced writers, instead of the more mature and seasoned reporters.

The beats I had worked on in the past decades required first, this very same town news; then the late night-early morning Hartford police beat; followed by daily all-state general news coverage; then reporting on all state courts; and finally, even more involved coverage of federal courts statewide.

After this demotion to the New Britain Bureau created a bit of workaholic depression, I retained an expert, specialized New Haven lawyer, Jacob "Jack" Zeldes. Decades earlier, he had first worked as a youthful news reporter for several years before becoming an attorney, occasionally accommodating newsmen.

He filed suit for me against The Courant in January 2003, alleging age discrimination.

Jack, as I came to call him, after receiving a small retainer and realizing my relatively modest salary, asked me to meet him inside a Hartford skyscraper office where he was advising another client.

As we gazed out on the sun dappled city, Jack offered to represent me without further fees. I was so thankful and amazed! But I immediately exclaimed that I would not quit that legal action until The Courant was forced to pay his fees.

Months later in 2004, The Courant gave in and compromised by allowing me to do part time investigative work while covering Middletown Superior Court. The Courant's settlement was without monetary damages for me, but paid for Attorney Zeldes' legal fees.

I will remember this compromise result for the rest of my life. It saved me from one of the worst daily nightmares of my career by demoting my news coverage from the excitement of corruption investigations to routine crime court coverage.

Minutes after the lawsuit compromise was arranged inside the Courant lawyer's high-rise Hartford office, a stone's throw from the newspaper, I thanked and tightly embraced Jack Zeldes on the street. I still feel that embrace! Indeed, that win was one of the greatest thrills for me ever! It calmed my bitterness at being demoted from my well recognized ability to work at length exposing corrupt activities in government, business and elsewhere.

CHAPTER 6

LIFE EXPERIENCES LEADING TO MY OWN INVESTIGATIVE REPORTING

Why was the victory of the lawsuit such a thrill? Not only had I worked intensively at The Courant for decades, but my major joy and purpose there had, over all those years, become investigations of government and business corruption. Once involved in such work, I could not turn back. It was clear to me that the desire and need to expose and publicize illegal, unethical and repulsive activities was in my blood.

I learned through intensive investigative experience that we here in the United States are living in a corpocracy, not a Democracy. The corporations rule our economy and our politics and have done so for at least since the 1890s and even more in early 1900s. Early attempts to control big corporations during that period and later, never became consistent enough to stop their domination of the economy and lobbying leaking constantly to weaken federal and state consumer protection laws.

More than once in a while, the people, in the name of fairness to all income classes, lower, middle and upper, need the protection of the government from greedy corporate heads and thoughtless businesspeople.

It seems neither the Republicans nor most of the Democrats (usually not the Conservatives) have stepped in to protect the working people: those who NEED their own salaries and benefits to survive.

The two parties are so busy fighting that they usually don't have the leadership to solve or lower the unemployment rates when they go out of control percentage wise.

Meanwhile, the bankers at the top and many of the corporate leaders and businessmen and women responsible are still making millions at the expense of those they are laying off who need a living wage to survive.

This is not about welfare. It is about caring enough for other people to allow them to become part of the regular working life equation. If the corporate world doesn't have the leadership to care about those competent people in the lower wage levels, the government becomes their only protection. But, obviously, that unemployment protection is not enough.

In the news business where I have worked in for the last 45 years, corporate heads have taken to laying off, buying out and firing newsmen, and, as a result, cutting the quality of their product.

Some of these corporate heads continue to raise their own, hopefully competent, dollar share of the product, news. In the meantime, a lot of the news quality has become low enough that journalists who care for in depth writing need to go to the Internet to search for freelance jobs, the pay rarely reflecting the many hours or days it takes to investigate the subject.

This corporate greed totally reduces the amount of in depth and investigative reporting, creating the incentive for more corruption in government and in business.

Meanwhile, news has become a TV and on-line system of talking heads (like Fox News). This means of reporting simply spreads gossip and false or questionable accusations attracting the worst of politicians, like Donald Trump, to join in and spread the emotional word to their fans.

So not only is true Democracy dying, but its politicians often ignore the Fourth Estate nationwide as a watchdog to keep government and business honest, making corpocracy even more powerful. Without valid public exposure, GREED rules!

See a copy of Truthout's in depth news story by me on this tragic subject in Scoop Independent News: http://www.scoop.co.nz/stories/HL0611/S00381.htm

"If some doomsday industry analysts are to be believed, newspapers are laid out and stacked neatly inside their own future death warehouses, not only in the United States, but worldwide."

Connecticut has been a fertile field for corruption for most of the forty years I worked at The Courant. The state became known as Corrupticut. The Courant itself confirmed that reputation in a February 2015 editorial by Stephen Busemeyer. Here is part of it:

"Political corruption in Connecticut is like this winter's snow: It just won't stop. Which is why federal agencies have to set up a serious stakeout here? "

"The U.S. attorney's office, the FBI and four other federal agencies are forming the Connecticut Public Corruption Task Force to root out all those who use their public position for private gain. The corruption tip hot line,1-800-CALL-FBI, operates 24/7."

"It's a sad commentary when the federal government feels a state merits its own round-the-clock corruption unit. In a way, federal investigators and prosecutors are doing what they have done here for years: taking the lead in draining corruption cesspools."

"The reason why it's fallen to them to watchdog Connecticut corruption is because the state legislature refuses to hand state prosecutors the tool to do it — the investigative subpoena, which would give them the power to compel witness testimony," said the Hartford Courant Editorial by Stephen Busemeyer, editorial writer. See http://www.courant.com/opinion/editorials/hc-ed-corrupticut-20150208-story.html

My own career at The Courant began in 1966, after over three years in the U.S. Army, mostly inside the Army Intelligence Corps. That military experience was absolutely quintessential, inspiring and apt for my later years as an investigative journalist. In fact, that military activity created a tough, unexpected series of adventures which unwittingly, indirectly and ultimately galvanized me into depth news writing that became my daily, weekly and yearly career.

CHAPTER 7

THREATS AND CHALLENGES TO MY CAREER

At the start of my investigative reporting career, I had never been seriously threatened by the subject of a story as it was progressing or even after one had broken with a Courant page one headline.

That streak ended when my colleague, Tom Condon, and I finished up separate detailed and nerve-racking probes of poor gambling enforcement and irregularities within the Bridgeport police department.

After we finished up our intense questioning of Police Superintendent Joseph Walsh about overall force irregularities, he threatened us. Walsh suggested we should seriously worry as a result of what he considered inaccuracies in our investigative work of the department and, as a result, what he considered our false conclusions.

The very Monday when the Courant's article appeared, obviously under orders from Superintendent Walsh, a police vehicle followed the news delivery truck around. When it stopped in sales locations, police purchased all of the papers so any potential news readers could not view the page one story about Superintendent Walsh. The story's headline was: ''Hard-Line Boss Helps Bridgeport Policemen Flout Rules.'' This amazing police cover up newspaper buying caused a suburban weekly to reprint the story.

In August 1981, more than six and a half years after our in-depth probe of those irregularities, FBI investigators developed their own suspicions of Superintendent Walsh. Federal prosecutors, as part of an investigation into the Bridgeport police, had been tipped that Walsh might be receptive to a bribe for a lucrative city towing contract. They set up a cooperative undercover agent to arrange a Bridgeport parking lot meeting with Walsh to offer him a $5,000 portion of a $30,000 bribe.

But, because the city police were suspicious of the undercover agent's past criminal record in advance, the attempt backfired.

A Hartford Courant article described the incident. After the agent handed the envelope of money to Superintendent Walsh, he exclaimed, "Now put your hands on the dashboard. You're under arrest for attempted bribery." Immediately and separately, both Walsh's nearby hidden policemen and the opposing FBI agents closed in.

Police arrived first to support Walsh and arrest the undercover federal agent. Immediately, then, incoming federal agents demanded the return of the money and the criminal monitoring equipment from the police, but they refused to cooperate.

After an initial burst of sensational publicity over this weird and wild episode, the complicated legal matter was settled quietly. The federal bribery charge was eliminated, and the money and equipment were returned by police to the FBI.

At a news conference, Mr. Walsh was quoted by The New York Times as saying: "I feel bad about the whole thing. I still don't believe there's room in this country for members of the Justice Department, members of the F.B.I., to act like Gestapo."

Suspicions about Walsh's fishy activities did not end.

Here is The New York Time's account published two years and three months after Walsh's extraordinary run in with those FBI agents who unsuccessfully set him up for a bribe.

The story appeared December 16, 1983 and was written by reporter Richard Madden.

"Joseph A. Walsh, Bridgeport's Superintendent of Police for the past 22 years, was forced into retirement this week, and his ouster came with the suddenness of a coup d'etat.

While Mr. Walsh was convalescing at home with a circulatory problem Tuesday night, the city's Board of Police Commissioners, heeding a request from Mayor Leonard S. Paoletta, voted 6 to 0 to retire the 67-year-old Superintendent.

Within a half-hour, the Mayor went on the police radio and announced: "Attention all police. Superintendent Walsh has been retired tonight. I am the chief law enforcement officer. Take your orders in the normal chain of command."

Private security guards were moved in to protect the Mayor and members of the police commission. "To make sure emotions didn't run amok," Mr. Paoletta explained later.

The action stunned some members of the Police Department. Mr. Walsh, a feisty chief who had been on the force for 42 years, said he would fight his forced retirement and would go to court, if necessary, to keep his job. "I will be back," he said in an interview at his home. "I don't run when I'm fighting."

Sure enough, seven months later, New York Time's Reporter Madden followed up with this story about Walsh's return following a legal battle.

''Mr. Walsh, 68 years old and a veteran of 42 years on the force, walked back into headquarters as head of the 400-member police department in Connecticut's largest city. A crowd of 50 supporters greeted him with a bouquet of gladiolas and a big cake inscribed: 'Welcome Home Super.'

After a court fight, Madden wrote, ''a state trial referee ruled that there was "no just cause" for Mr. Walsh's dismissal.''

The Times article ended with this striking conclusion. ''Although Mr. Walsh was back on the job last week, he was not entirely in charge. The Mayor and the police commissioners said they would monitor the department daily. The superintendent was also told he would need the Mayor's permission for every purchase over $50. Mr. Walsh, however, savored his return. He said of his ouster, "I still have resentments against those who did that, but I won't let it interfere."

Even better for the miraculous Walsh combatant, in August 1986, three years after his fights with the city began, he won $420,000 in a lawsuit's damages from a Superior Court judgment over all those battles for his job with Bridgeport officials.

Tom Condon's and my reporting on Walsh and his out of the ordinary activities in the police department were the kind of lengthy, controversial in-depth news work, related to Editor Irving Kravsow's supervision of me. It became more and more inspiring as the years at The Courant passed.

Here is what The Courant wrote about Irving in his October 6, 2013 obituary:

''Though he held other positions as well, Irving M. Kravsow was the archetypal editor: feisty, savvy, well-connected, hard driving. He brought those qualities to The Courant's news operation for four decades after World War II.''

I remember one episode in particular in which Irving's thoughtful fairness saved me from further trouble. He had a three-dimensional understanding of the news and his reporters.

"He was the most memorable part of a management culture that encouraged every reporter to be an investigator on behalf of the public, including those suspects passing through the court system," wrote Andrew Kreig, one of the many in-depth reporters who worked for Irving over the years.

The Kravsow episode came at a time when my father, a well-known antique dealer, and his good friend, a congenial pharmacist, were working together to save the historical Litchfield Superior Court from being abandoned.

At that very time, I was working on an in-depth story or two with veteran staff crime reporter Gerald "Gerry" Demeusy, involving the controversial backup, delay and accumulation of civil court cases.

One of the most powerful jurists in the state, whose name I will not mention because he passed away years ago and I do not want to aggravate his loved ones, was responsible for working on such controversies.

It so happened that one day I was inside the Crutch & MacDonald Pharmacy, entirely separate from Dad's visit there. He was conversing with his pharmacist partner while they were battling authorities to keep the state Superior Court in an historic building right in the very center of Litchfield. I was inside the drug store separately, probably buying a New York Times.

To the best of my memory that long ago, Dad, since deceased, must have seen me before I even knew he was there. He always had a big, spontaneous sense of humor. He loved to joke about people the family knew and especially current events. Dad was NEVER a malicious joker. So, as he was talking with his save-the-court – pharmacist partner, he spotted me and shouted out humorously: "I want justice, not Justice X " (last name retracted)!

Of course, the relevance of that remark to Dad and his friend the pharmacist was this. That very powerful state judge was one of those planning the possibility of that local, historical court being abandoned in favor of a brand new one in Torrington, the judge's home town, several miles away.

Not long thereafter, the next morning, while I was still home, I received a telephone call from that very same judge, complaining to me about Dad's joking exclamation of his name, and my presence when he did so. I apologized profusely, but said I had nothing whatsoever to do with that remark.

But, subsequently, when I got to work at the Courant, Irving Kravsow, immediately and loudly exclaimed out from his office into the newsroom, "Dennie, get in here!"

I, naturally, obeyed. Irving immediately told me about the judge's complaint to him regarding Dad's drug store exclamation about him. With trepidation, right away, I told Irving I had nothing to do with that comment, and until the remark itself happened, was unaware Dad was in the pharmacy. Although upset, Irving forgave me, and allowed my continued court coverage.

Much later, I was having lunch outside with my wife, Ina, at a Washington, Connecticut, restaurant, the George Washington Tavern, when I spotted that very same judge sitting with guests at a large table below.

Behind them were a series of tall fire burning lanterns. At one point, I spotted the judge talking to his next chair associate and pointing a finger up toward me. Immediately, I assumed he was talking about the earlier episode so upsetting him.

Then, as I was about to leave, I looked down at his table and greeted him by name in a loud, stirring voice. He immediately stood up and began walking along the line of flaming lamps with his back relatively close to them. I was concerned and exclaimed a loud warning.

When he finally arrived face-to-face with me, the judge said, with slight humor in his voice, "Dennie, you always had the fire to my back!" I, of course, instantly disagreed, saying essentially: 'No your honor, I would never do such a thing."

This is the court operations story involving that judge and the legal system Demeusy and I investigated and wrote after weeks of work.

Judges, Court Staff Declare State Judicial System Crumbling
December 30, 1979

"
—

CHAPTER 8

CONNECTICUT CONTRACTORS USE PHONY COMPANIES TO CHEAT A LAW BENEFITING ACTUAL MINORITY FIRMS

One day in July 1980 while I was still assigned as a daily state-wide court reporter, a Courant reporter I then barely knew, Dick Lehr, unexpectedly paid me a visit inside Hartford Superior Court.

That unexpected visit occurred while I was covering a well-known African American crook whose name escapes me. Lehr pulled me aside in the big court hallway and told me this guy operates one of a number of minority front businesses in the construction industry which fronts for one of the big million-dollar construction companies.

I didn't have any idea what Dick was discussing. He then enthusiastically asked me to come back to The Courant and he would explain.

So when I got back, Dick told me to get on one phone and listen in on our call to another of these front companies, called Atkinson Builders. It pretended to be an independent firm, but actually was a secret illicit partner of one of the biggest construction companies in Connecticut, O&G Industries. So Dick dialed up the number and after a few rings, a woman answered like this: "O&G Industry....noooo! Atkinson Builders!"

I almost dropped the phone on the floor. Dick Lehr, as I remember, was already off and laughing harder than he usually did!

Not long afterward, we were off and running! We both drove out to check out a road reconstruction site in Torrington. While there, we spotted an Atkinson Builders pickup truck on a small hill sticking out purposefully for all to see. Then, we soon spotted a big African American worker on top of a huge yellow piece of road-building equipment, working on the highway.

Lehr then exclaimed: "Hey Dennie! You smoke, right?! Go over to that machinery and hail to the guy and climb up on it. Ask him for a cigarette!" So being an obedient partner, I did just what Dick Lehr told me to do.

The guy stopped the machine. I climbed up there and asked him for a cigarette, which he indeed gave me. Then I asked him if he worked for Atkinson Builders and he started laughing and said something like "What Atkinson Builders?" That, I could tell from this obvious construction site participant was essentially the implied message from him. In other words, the company did not exist.

So later that day, we waited for the Atkinson pickup truck to leave and followed it home to the address of an O&G supervisor. That, of course, was only the beginning of the story which hit the paper after we had proven several other fronts for its factual basis.

And guess what, after that minority front story, I did another one like it with Cliff Teutsch, who later became the managing editor, and then the editor of the paper before he passed away in October 2014.

After we teamed up on this fascinating corrupt pattern of well-known Connecticut contractors taking advantage of diminutive minority businesses, Dick Lehr left The Courant to work at the Boston Globe.

He then became even more involved with in depth reporting focused on government corruption and its intertwine with well-known mobster activities. Eventually, he wrote more than a half dozen books including one with Gerard O'Neill that became a fascinating movie about true to life mobster activities, called "Black Mass."

Here is the minority-front investigative piece I wrote with Dick Lehr.

White-Owned Companies Abuse Minority Contractors Programs
July 20, 1980

CHAPTER 9

CORRUPTION SPREADS OVER THE YEARS IN HARTFORD PROBATE COURT

One of the most exciting news investigations I ever worked on, and one which riveted many news readers for years, involved malfeasance within the Hartford Probate Court, ruled by Judge James H. Kinsella.

The court was then located in City Hall center city at 550 Main Street, but inspired little news or reporters' visits for years. Its judge had powerful authority over the management of deceased persons' estates as well as those for the mentally incompetent. At that time, the court's reach included not just Hartford, but also affluent West Hartford, now with its own court since January 2011.

One of the most fascinating news investigation spotlights I ever worked under, arose from checking into multiple episodes of malfeasance within that very Hartford court before the split system change. This imperious judge ruled that court, relied upon by many mentally vulnerable and incompetent rich elderly people, for 24 years.

Before his controversial court activities, Kinsella, who died in October 2012, had been an influential city official. First he was a councilman for eight years, then a deputy mayor, and finally a mayor for two terms from 1957 to 1960. That very last year, after retiring as mayor, he then ran for and was elected probate judge.

He attracted little public attention for years. But, as time wore on, amazingly, two decades later, in the early 1980s, his repetitious unscrupulous judicial activities began creating story after story reported extensively by myself and another reporter in The Courant, Mark Stillman. Those investigative and regular news pieces dramatically and ultimately forced him out of office in 1984.

That year Kinsella became the first Connecticut official in state history to face impeachment for unscrupulous government operations. It was then, decades earlier, that impeachment was first established in the Connecticut Constitution. Ultimately, probe after probe forced Kinsella to resign before the State Senate could hold a trial to decide his fate.

The State House of Representatives had already recommended Kinsella's impeachment on May 1, 1984, sending the case on to The Senate for trial evidence and testimony. Two days later, before the

Senate could take on the House referral, Kinsella resigned, ending that legislative impeachment effort.

Three years earlier, the initial focus of The Courant's Kinsella investigations, uncannily, became temporarily delayed when Staff Reporter Mark Stillman discovered that unknowingly, by chance, both he and I were focused upon the same news target.

We immediately agreed to coordinate. And, amazingly, Mark and I then worked off and on for three years of intensive digging. A particularly crucial moment arrived while we were researching Superior Court records together in an office for hours. We finally discovered the first dramatic and crucial conflict of interest, implicating Kinsella and Attorney Alexander A. Goldfarb, who died in 1987.

Here is my news partner Mark Stillman's analysis of the news business, leading to our seemingly endless investigation, back in those days.

"One of the big problems with the Courant as well as other newspapers in the 1980s was keeping reporters on a very tight leash. Editors prevented a writer from published comments, no matter how obvious and truthful. All critical words needed the backing of documents or attribution a source. Reporters were almost discouraged from using their logical thoughts in writing."

"However, this is a book," Mark explained. "The Courant is not now in editing control. An author can use his own discretion as to his truth and accuracy."

Mark continued: "Now is the time to talk about what it was like for myself and Dennie, to work on and write about these stories. Now this writer, Dennie, needs to honestly deal in his own writing as it relates to Courant editors. It is this writer alone who must candidly interact with people involved with all his stories, including both the helpful sources and the hostile targets. "

"The readers want to know," wrote Mark, " what goes on behind the scenes, not just what is printed in the newspaper. Unless the author tells them, they will have no clue as to what it is like to set up for, and then conduct, a confrontation interview."

"They won't know what it's like to deal with the opinions of editors and then the legal opinions of the newspaper's lawyer who was Ralph Elliot," said Mark." They won't know what it's like to deal with regular news sources or politicians who are constantly lying to you or what effect it has on you, after a while of absorbing all that talk."

"Additionally," Mark continued, "those readers also won't know the special trust that your sources, sometimes total strangers, have in you as a reporter. Remember: they tell you information that, if anyone else knew they were your source, it could easily cost them their jobs, get them sued, or otherwise ruin their lives."

In the Ethel Donaghue story, concerning the millionaire woman whose estate became a battle of lawyers pilling up legal fees, we talked to a lot of her household staff. They had everything to lose from talking to us, and nothing to gain except - to vindicate a sense of justice; or to right the incredible wrongs that had been done to their mistress, Miss Donaghue. They and others almost always called her Miss Donaghue.

Because Miss Donaghue had treated her household employees kindly and courteously, they went out on a limb for her.

But, what about Alexander A. Goldfarb, her court compelled lawyer and James Kinsella, the probate judge? They were eminently capable of taking cruel advantage of an elderly woman, who was all alone in the world with no close relatives but loads of money.

I too have now thought deeply about the Goldfarb-Kinsella matter, and a little bit about reporting in general.

Here are just some of the observations I've made: The reputations of these two well-known professional legal creatures, Kinsella and Goldfarb, were harmed by the Donaghue matter. I'm sure after the stories broke, they had trouble holding their heads up high to the outside world, especially in Hartford or the State of Connecticut.

Indeed, they must have had to hide from shame. That has to be a crushing blow. That was especially true for someone like Goldfarb who basked in any kind of admiration or attention; who loved to see his name in print; and who had an extraordinarily inflated narcissistic image of himself.

We, the reporters, did not destroy their professional reputations. They did, at least in serious part. And it was almost a fluke happening. For years, they had gotten away with their shenanigans. We, the news reporters, remember Goldfarb's favorite bar and restaurant in Hartford, in the Bushnell Plaza development where he lived.

It was called Shenanigans. We went there for lunch with him at his proud suggestion, however reluctantly. After all, it was to be the day of our confrontation interview. There was no obvious reason for Goldfarb to suspect anything deeply worrying about our probe. He did expect a detailed news interview at this point.

Goldfarb and Kinsella had relied for years on the naivete, credulity, and utter one-dimensional queries from local reporters. Goldfarb knew if from time to time he kept feeding the reporters some colorful quotes about routine "news" matters involving state politics, or city government, for example, that would keep them satisfied and happy.

They would not dare, he thought, bite the hand that fed them. Most reporters wanted his colorful quotes and friendly access to keep on coming. It is so much easier gathering news that way.

A few years before these in-depth stories all broke, I remember meeting Bill Clew, by then retired from the Courant, where he had been managing editor and thus my boss.

One day, Reporter Marc Gunther and I ran into Clew inside the hallways of the state Freedom of Information Commission, where he had become a commissioner. Gunther and I were constantly bringing Freedom of Information complaints against the Town of Manchester, which we then covered.

I remember Gunther asking Mr. Clew for any advice he might have for us as reporters. His advice was simple and straightforward: "just keep on plugging away. Go into Town Hall every day and check with all the departments, even the little-known ones."

I remember distinctly he mentioned the local probate courts as an example of an often-neglected office for news coverage. That seemed like strange and useless advice, but I began to think thought about it, so it remained in the back of my mind.

In Manchester, the state had a probate court, of course, and I walked by it every day, as it was right next to the hearing room where the town council held its meetings. But I had never gone inside and knew nothing about it.

It was only a few years later, while I was covering the City of Hartford, that we got the tip about the potential of hot irregularity news inside the Hartford Probate Court.

Yet, for years, TV and print reporters covering Hartford City Hall had walked by the Probate Court offices every weekday never to go inside. We probably would not have learned much about intricate operations from the judge. Had we gone inside court, Kinsella, spotting us and discovering we were investigative reporters, would have made sure of that.

But if we had poked our heads in occasionally, and kept our eyes and ears open ... who knows? Perhaps the legal attorney 'foxes' would not have dared challenge those 'news boys residing in the silly newsroom,' as many lawyers described us as.

However, the mere thought that reporters might be regularly watching, might have acted as a temporary check on Kinsella and Goldfarb. Although knowing them and their increasing brazenness ... I doubt it. And remember, reporters come and go, and newspapers' institutional memories are often ephemeral. The pressures of publishing daily news stories create that. But, what about Kinsella and Goldfarb? Memories of their public wonder were regular - or so they thought.

Now back I go to how Mark's and my initial probes continued. Our investigation found a court document showing that Goldfarb and Kinsella had been co-counsels on a case. In addition, the small law office Kinsella worked out of was in a compact building near Hartford's center for which Goldfarb was trustee.

Research revealed at one point that they had the same telephone number. Indeed, we later wrote an investigative article on Goldfarb's questionable handling of another estate's wills. It was then that we wrote, without subsequent objection, that Goldfarb and Kinsella were not only close friends, but had been law associates.

Nevertheless, at one point, Goldfarb insisted, "We were just sharing offices. We had no arrangement. Everything was separate. We had different clients, different secretaries… different phone numbers."

Indeed, we when wrote an investigative article on Goldfarb's questionable handling of another estate's will, we mentioned without subsequent denials from either Goldfarb and Kinsella regarding their close personal and fiscal relationships.

The flamboyant Goldfarb himself was a prominent state Democratic politician. He had for several years been Hartford Corporation Counsel and was a confidant of Connecticut Governor Ella Grasso.

Our investigation revealed that a court document showed Goldfarb and Kinsella had been co-counsels on a legal case in a court unrelated to probate. As well, the small law office Kinsella worked out of was in a compact building, near Hartford's center, for which structure Goldfarb was trustee. Research revealed they even had the same telephone number.

Not only did Kinsella, also a Democratic activist, have a regular law practice, but as probate judge, he was repeatedly appointing Goldfarb as a lawyer or conservator, fiscally ministering for elderly rich people who couldn't care for their own finances.

In one case, then not yet in probate, Goldfarb took over the will writing affairs of O. Hope Baxter, a task previously handled by a lawyer in Kinsella's firm. Goldfarb said that firm, despite his personal relationship with Kinsella, did not represent a conflict because Kinsella was not involved. Baxter had put all of her fiscal affairs in Goldfarb's hands.

About a year after he wrote Baxter's first replacement will, leaving most of her belongings to her friends and former employees, Goldfarb told her that the will was inadequate.

Ultimately, months later, in July 1978, Goldfarb drafted another will leaving all of Baxter's tangible property to himself. That, records showed, excluded bonds, bank accounts, treasury certificates, securities and cash. She had made Goldfarb trustee of other valuables and conservator of her estate.

The value of her endowment cannot be easily estimated; although in 1972 she received an inheritance conservatively valued at $156,000 and owned other property worth at least $100,000. Earlier, she had given Goldfarb an oil painting attributed to the 17th century artist Meindert Hobbema, which if authentic, would be worth as much as $150,000.

Asked if he knew the painting was authentic before he received it, Goldfarb said, "I really didn't care because I'm not interested in the painting." He said he agreed orally with Baxter to give the painting to the Wadsworth Atheneum upon his death.

If a lawyer is to be given such assets by a client, the Connecticut Code of Professional Responsibility says: when clients propose to give assets to their attorney, they must first secure disinterested advice from an independent person. Goldfarb said he did not urge that Baxter get such advice. When we interviewed him, Goldfarb insisted, he would decline the assets left him in that will.

In two interviews with The Courant, Baxter said that she no longer wanted to leave Goldfarb anything and was sick as hell when that will was prepared. She had a serious eye operation in 1974. Her doctors refused to talk to the Courant about her health.

In other cases - talk about lucrative work - records show Goldfarb took in $400,000 in probate fees for scores of court appointments awarded by his close buddy, Kinsella, who approved those fees as probate judge.

Still another of those cases involved the $32 million estate of a West Hartford lady and retired lawyer, 84-year-old Ethel Frances Donaghue. She had been declared unfit to handle her fortune by Kinsella. The funds accumulated from an inheritance and her earnings. She lived alone in an exclusive part of West Hartford, on the same street as the official state's Governor's Mansion.

Her situation became a headlined inside a March 4, 1981 Courant investigative story, by-lined by Mark Stillman and myself. Mark wrote the story, needing little or no editing, after we had both investigated.

Donaghue's original lawyer was William W. Graulty. But his control was altered in January 1979 when Kinsella declared her legally incompetent because of failing health.

Kinsella then made Graulty and Goldfarb as Donaghue's co-conservators in the estate, and Hartford Attorney Paul J. Aparo, a former clerk in Kinsella's court, to watch over them. These lawyers were overseeing the largest estate ever placed under conservatorship in Hartford and one of the largest ever seen by local banks.

From that fortune, during the first 1 ½ years of the conservatorship, Aparo received $38,071 in fees, Graulty $166,267 and Goldfarb $165,200. Including these fees they had spent about $500,000 a year on the estate. Expenditures authorized by Goldfarb included $40,000 for a new Mercedes car on behalf of a wheel-chaired lady, $87,000 for landscaping services and $14,000 for parties at the Donaghue estate.

During a two-and-a-half-year period, the record showed Goldfarb's and Graulty's fees together exceeded $500,000.

Speaking of potential conflicts, Donaghue's initial will, drafted by Graulty, left all of Donaghue's fortune to a charitable corporation whose directors included Graulty and his wife, his law partner and two bankers who formerly worked under Graulty in the trust department of the Connecticut Bank & Trust Co.

The investigative news of Goldfarb's controversial appointment soon forced Kinsella to disqualify himself and submit to a takeover by Judge Ralph D. Lukens. The judge subsequently removed both Goldfarb and Graulty, who between the two of them had made a controversial total of $250,000 in fees.

As an aside, "the Donaghue estate was one of more 40 probate appointments given to Mr. Goldfarb over the years, earning him a total of more than $500,000 in legal fees. Conduct 'Brought Disdain,' " says The New York Times.

https://www.nytimes.com/1984/05/03/nyregion/impeachment-move-sets-precedent-in-connecticut.html

Takeover Judge Lukens simultaneously called for a probate council probe of Kinsella's conduct, leading to his censure.

Ultimately, it was that very case that prompted six state representatives to call for a State House of Representative probe, eventually resulting in Kinsella's impeachment investigation.

"When they met in the Statehouse here in 1818, the drafters of Connecticut's Constitution provided that all executive and judicial officials were subject to impeachment. Only now, 166 years later, is their mandate being put to use," said the New York Times.

After considering the evidence, the House voted to impeach Kinsella on May 1, 1984, but he resigned before the Senate could take over for a trial of the House's resolution.

A state legal grievance complaint brought against Goldfarb and Graulty for their handling of the Donaghue case was dismissed by Superior Court Judge Norris O'Neill and appealed by the state but dropped after Goldfarb died in 1987.

However, The Council on Probate Judicial Conduct had found this strong ethical critique of their actions in the Ethel Donaghue case:

"There was sufficient evidence to find, by clear and convincing proof, that Goldfarb had private communications with Judge Kinsella about the Donaghue estate, and that his tenure as co-conservator resulted from favoritism by Judge Kinsella rather than from an objective appraisal of the needs of the Donaghue estate."

In the midst of a March 4, 1985 court hearing in that case, O'Neill, amazingly, jailed State Rep. Christopher Shays for contempt after he refused to leave the witness stand while objecting to proceedings, he considered regrettable.

Shays, who contended that the lawyers received excessive fees from the estate, said at the hearing that he wanted to make a statement before Judge O'Neill to protest the slow pace of the disciplinary proceedings.

But, O'Neill, based on Shays' interruption, instead forced an extraordinary contempt of court penalty that eventually forced Shays to spend seven days in jail before being released.

For two years, Shays had been campaigning for disciplinary action against Goldfarb, Graulty and Kinsella for their handling of the $38 million estate

Some insisted O'Neill had a political bias for Kinsella that made his ability to impartially preside over the case impossible. Others said O'Neill was one of the few to remain independent and levelheaded in the midst of the scandal's inertia.

Shays was quoted out of court as saying there is a local "club of lawyers and judges who have become so ingrown that they don't carry out the responsibility they have to the general public." He was the first official to call for Kinsella's impeachment. Years later, Shays, totally unimpeded by his jailing, and instead enhanced, was elected to the U.S. Congress.

Even a daily and crucial probate court worker for Kinsella became active the court's irregular activities. The Courant repeatedly exposed the activities of probate court investigator Abraham "Al" Cohen. He was ultimately arrested and later convicted in U.S District Court in May 1983 of perjury. Cohen was then sentenced to three months in prison and fined $3,500.

He had been lying about his recollections of an oriental rug that belonged to a West Hartford estate. Cohen received a $10,000 fee as Kinsella-appointed temporary administrator of that estate and $1,083 for selling off the estate's furnishings including the rug.

Kinsella, himself, escaped scrutiny for his supervision of Cohen's irregular court activities. He died October 8, 2012, while Goldfarb passed away in September 1987.

The most publicized of Kinsella's court irregularities was the Ethel Donaghue case. Here is the background of that very case in an investigative Hartford Courant story I wrote, exposing the intricate details of that very contentious probate court case, after months of investigation.

FEES BEING QUESTIONED IN INHERITANCE CASEI

THOMAS D. WILLIAMS; Courant Staff Writer THE HARTFORD COURANT

Fifteen years after wrangling over the Ethel Donaghue estate brought notoriety to some prominent Hartford lawyers, the attorney for one of her heirs is being asked to justify his fees for handling the inheritance.

The Manchester lawyer, Vincent L. Diana, is responsible for protecting Thomas R. Finnegan's interest in Donaghue's estate.

He has charged Finnegan, a 65-year-old disabled Navy veteran whose mother, Edith, was related to Donaghue's mother, $98,624 in fees, or 30 percent of the inheritance.

Shirley Pagluica, a town social service worker charged with looking after Finnegan's personal affairs, questioned the size of Diana's fee and the propriety of his legal assistant's getting paid for improvements to Finnegan's house.

A hearing was held on the dispute in April but was suspended to discuss a settlement. No new hearing date has been set.

Diana, the Hartford County Bar Association's president-elect, and Pagluica are co-conservators, appointed by the town's probate judge to manage, respectively, Finnegan's financial and personal affairs. His estate, including his house, is worth about $750,000.

Donaghue, who died Dec. 30, 1989, at 93, was a West Hartford resident and one of the first female lawyers to appear before the U.S. Supreme Court. After a court dispute over her various wills, Donaghue's estate, worth a total of $66 million, left Finnegan $363,000.

Donaghue's estate became the subject of a prolonged controversy 15 years ago. Hundreds of thousands of dollars in legal fees and expenses were assessed against the estate while Donaghue was incapable of handling her affairs. That led to state and federal investigations of several lawyers and others involved in the estate.

Two lawyers -- Alexander A. Goldfarb and William W. Graulty -- were removed as Donaghue's conservators, and a third -- Paul J. Aparo -- was removed as guardian. The probate judge who supervised the case, James H. Kinsella, was censured and retired rather than face impeachment.

Donaghue's cousin, Finnegan, had a mental breakdown in the Navy. After his release in the early 1950s, he was cared for first by his father, now deceased, and then by a hired housekeeper, said Robert D. Harrison, a longtime friend of the family's.

Harrison said he is one of several people in town upset about Diana's fees. "In my opinion, I don't think that [the fees] are either fair or just. It seems terribly excessive to me," Harrison said.

He also cited payment to Diana's legal assistant, June A. Fields, for supervising the estate's spending of about $30,000 to renovate, furnish and clean Finnegan's house. Fields would not comment.

Pagluica protested to Manchester Probate Judge William E. FitzGerald earlier this year.

When Diana was asked to justify his legal fees, he said FitzGerald had informally approved the arrangement without a hearing.

The judge then disqualified himself because he became a potential witness. The court file shows FitzGerald denied approving the fees.

State rules for lawyers require that the kind of contingency fee Diana received be put in writing and approved in advance. That was not done on Finnegan's case.

FitzGerald, Diana and Pagluica have declined comment.

A replacement judge, George G. McManus, recommended a compromise to save Finnegan the legal fees it could cost him to resolve the matter. Court records show Diana agreed to refund $13,000 of the $98,624 to settle the case. McManus still would have to approve that arrangement and the home-improvement expenses, after a hearing.

Diana's fee, which is 25 percent higher than the U.S. Veterans Administration recommends for legal fees in the cases of disabled veterans, draws varying opinions from lawyers in the Donaghue dispute. Conrad O. Seifert, an Old Lyme attorney for three other Donaghue relatives, said before Finnegan's hearing was suspended, he was ready to testify the fee was "excessive and unreasonable," because Diana did not appear at the Donaghue hearings and took the fee without formal court approval.

Diana sent an associate, Diane S. Prior, to the Donaghue hearings, which consumed about 10 days. Prior spent most of her time as a spectator and largely relied on the legal arguments and research of several other lawyers, court witnesses say.

Seifert said he was one of the few lawyers who examined witnesses and argued the case. His fee, paid by his three clients, was $39,000.

Because he recovered $1 million, Seifert said, his clients gave him a $21,000 bonus, so his total fee for each client was $20,000.

Two other lawyers in the Donaghue case disagreed with Seifert. They said Diana was entitled to the 30 percent cut of Finnegan's inheritance, so long as his fees were approved by the court.

CHAPTER 10

UGLY PRISON CONDITIONS INSPIRE IN DEPTH PROBE

Almost a decade after those probate court exposures, in July 1992, my investigative work moved on to the incredibly unprofessional handling of state prison inmates.

Similar to my own analysis, Colin Poitras believed Connecticut's correctional system in the early 1990s needed a close investigative news look, so as a typical example, we chose to focus on the inappropriately named Cheshire Correctional Center.

Here are his detailed thoughts now about our probe more than two and a half decades after the story was published.

''I think the biggest impact of that story was the change in prison management to a more humane treatment model."

''We wrote that story when Connecticut's prison population was bursting at the seams. People were stacked like firewood. Basically, as I remember, our story exposed that practice and got them to change. No more overloading cells. No more converting common areas to prisoner housing. No one exposed that before.''

''Perhaps in the long run, it motivated the state to upgrade its older prisons like Cheshire Correctional, which were dangerous and unhealthy for inmates. It also may have contributed to the movement that led the state to change its sentencing policies. ''

"The prison population has been steadily declining.''

After an intricate investigation, here's the story we wrote.

THOMAS D. WILLIAMS and COLIN POITRAS; Courant Staff Writers. Hartford Courant; Hartford, Conn. [Hartford, Conn] 04 July 1992: c1.

Reports show poor conditions at prison Reports reveal trouble at Cheshire prison: [An Edition]

The problems in the 22-cell segregation unit are part of a larger story at Cheshire, a 72-year-old prison where several inmates have complained about conditions. State officials concede conditions at Cheshire fall short of other prisons statewide.

Insufficient health services -- Inpatient and outpatient mental health services at Cheshire and state prisons and jails other than Niantic, [Somers] and the Manson Youth Institution are "slim to non-existent," correction budget reports say. A dearth of health-care staffing at Cheshire and some other institutions threatens to violate the state's health code, the budget reports explain.

At Cheshire, the prison medical staff meets many inmates' routine medical needs but cannot provide advanced care to inmates with substantial health problems, such as AIDS or serious mental illness. Correction officials estimate that statewide, 15 percent of prisoners are HIV-positive, and [Warden Leonard Barbieri] said he believes that figure is accurate for Cheshire.

The most violent inmates in the Cheshire prison are often doubled up in 9-by-6-foot, sparsely lit cells in the prison's segregation unit. One inmate sleeps on a single bunk and the other on a mattress wedged between the steel door and the toilet.

These convicts often spend 23 hours a day breathing stale air. They have few recreational, educational or vocational opportunities. The metal bunk bed is the only furniture.

The problems in the 22-cell segregation unit are part of a larger story at Cheshire, a 72-year-old prison where several inmates have complained about conditions. State officials concede conditions at Cheshire fall short of other prisons statewide.

Monthly reports for 1991-92 by Warden Leonard Barbieri and his predecessors, Victor Liburdi and Edward Arrington, as well as other correction documents, reveal overcrowding, fire-code violations, inmate violence and poor inmate health care at Cheshire, a prison that is one security level below Somers, the state's only maximum-security prison.

In June, Cheshire inmate Peter Ventura, a 35-year-old convict who had been in the prison's segregation unit for more than six months, filed a lawsuit in U.S. District Court in New Haven claiming the prison violated his and other inmates' civil rights.

Ventura, who has seen other parts of the prison and also spent time at the Somers prison, said he considers the overall Cheshire environment "subhuman."

"It traumatizes you emotionally and mentally," Ventura said. "I felt like an animal and I've watched some inmates become animals because of it. They lash out at one another, at the guards, and the guards lash out at them."

Ventura, serving a 30-year sentence for sexual assault, is seeking a court order to correct unhealthy and dangerous conditions, which he said keep inmates from living in a safe and healthy environment.

This is not Ventura's first lawsuit. Several years ago, he filed a federal lawsuit against the staff and inmates at Somers that remains unresolved.

Inmates and guards at Cheshire have lived with outdated fire protection systems, violence, stale air and unhealthy conditions for decades. The 1991-92 warden's records and correction department documents reveal a litany of problems at Cheshire.

Here they are.

The segregation unit: Inmates are sent to segregation, built in the 1960s, for rules violations, assaults, inability to mix with other inmates and for their own protection. They are supposed to be there for no more than 30 days, although they can stay on for repeat violations. Ventura and two other inmates told reporters they spent months in segregation; Barbieri says that in each of those cases, special circumstances left him with little choice but to keep the men in segregation.

Outside air flows into these windowless cells -- comparable in size to a walk-in closet -- when guards open a slot in the solid steel door usually reserved for feedings.

The mattresses laid out next to the toilets are rolled up during the day to give inmates some semblance of room. Ventura and other inmates complain that the toilets can leak or splash over when toilets in other cells are flushed.

A wan, yellow light and a vent are hidden behind protective grates; a small sink sits in the corner. During the day, hazy light penetrates the Plexiglas skylight.

Somers prison, built in 1963, has a segregation unit that is much different. Instead of having the solid steel doors as Cheshire's cells do, Somers' barred cells face a wall with opaque windows. Each cell has a table and a chair, a large, recessed light, a big air vent, a recessed mirror, two bunk beds with drawers underneath and shelves.

Fire code: Until recently, Cheshire had not been inspected by the state fire marshal in four years. During a 1987 and 1988 inquiry, inspectors cited 36 fire safety violations.

Because the fire marshal's office is short-staffed, the warden was given up to five years to correct the violations.

After an inquiry by reporters into violations, the fire marshal returned to Cheshire in June. The prison had 13 violations, including lack of proper fire doors, and no fire alarm, sprinkler or smoke-detection systems in parts of the prison.

A similar delayed fire-code correction schedule was in place at the Bridgeport Correctional Center on July 3, 1990, when a century-old wing was gutted by fire, displacing 383 inmates.

Crowded population: Cheshire's average capacity last year was 832. Because of a lack of cell space, five to 15 inmates a week sleep on mattresses on the floor of the recreation rooms in the prison's South Block. In addition, the cells in the block, which were used routinely for one inmate each, now hold two.

Insufficient health services -- Inpatient and outpatient mental health services at Cheshire and state prisons and jails other than Niantic, Somers and the Manson Youth Institution are "slim to non-existent," correction budget reports say. A dearth of health-care staffing at Cheshire and some other institutions threatens to violate the state's health code, the budget reports explain.

An example of this is contained in warden's reports. In August 1991, a guard was assaulted by a mentally unbalanced inmate who had not taken his medication in at least two months.

At Cheshire, the prison medical staff meets many inmates' routine medical needs but cannot provide advanced care to inmates with substantial health problems, such as AIDS or serious mental illness. Correction officials estimate that statewide, 15 percent of prisoners are HIV-positive, and Barbieri said he believes that figure is accurate for Cheshire.

The medical ward, a small office and waiting room, is supervised by two doctors, two part-time psychiatrists and a dentist who also serves other prisons. Unlike Somers, there is no infirmary, so Cheshire prisoners with serious illnesses must either be sent to Somers or taken to a hospital.

Earlier state budget reductions had eliminated annual state health department inspections of cells, corridors and the rest of prison space. State Correction Commissioner Larry R. Meachum told legislators that further cuts "would have a dramatic impact not only in our facilities but will also pose major public health risks as inmates are released."

Violence: One of the Cheshire prison's main problems is mental stress for guards, the warden's reports indicate. For example, because of a number of gang-related incidents in April 1991, the prison staff was tense until the latter part of the month, when inmate leaders were identified and separated. Inmate morale, like staff morale, suffered because of gang difficulties, the warden reported.

Cheshire's 209 guards logged 43,938 overtime hours prison wide during the 12 months ending in June 1991. Overtime is necessary to quell disorders and replace guards injured on the job.

Between August and October 1991, the hours special officers spent investigating inmates' disciplinary problems, including alleged attacks by inmates on guards, increased 27 percent, from 58 to 74 hours per week.

Stuffy cell block: Inmates and correction officials say the prison's South Block has occasionally become so warm that inmates or staff broke windows to get cooler air. In the winter, those same windows were stuffed with cloth to keep out the cold.

The conditions that Ventura's lawsuit complains about could be changed if the state is able to complete a construction project at Cheshire.

Today, Cheshire's prisoners live in three main areas. There is the massive, 4-story-tall, steel-barred North Block, where 400 prisoners are alone in 7-by-5-foot cells; the South Block, where about 200 prisoners are doubled up in 8-by-6-foot cells; and two temporary dormitories, where another 200 inmates sleep in rows of beds in two large open rooms.

But two 300-unit cell blocks are expected to replace the antiquated North Block and the temporary dormitories; the first cell block is slated to open in September and the second by January 1993.

"I think the Department of Correction and the people here at Cheshire have taken a building that was built at the turn of the century for youthful offenders and managed an adult population through an overcrowding crisis of the 1980s and 1990s," Barbieri said. "The new construction at Cheshire is not only necessary, but it reflects good planning in providing for the state's needs into the 20th century."

Cells in the new blocks will be bigger -- 10-by-8 -- but inmates will continue to be doubled up in most of them. The prison also will gain a new 20-bed infirmary to Cheshire, but it will serve prisoners from throughout southern Connecticut.

As for the segregation unit, Barbieri said he has not decided whether he will replace the old unit when the new cell blocks open.

State Correction Commissioner Larry R. Meachum has said building prison space is not a cure-all, because there is no guarantee the state legislature will continue to provide the money to operate the additional cells. In fact, the number of guards and other workers needed at Cheshire, which with the new cell blocks will have an additional 500 prisoners, is not yet established.

Ventura, who recently was transferred to a New Haven jail as he nears trial on another assault charge, says he plans to see through his lawsuit against Cheshire.

"The staff here knows about these problems," Ventura said. "They tell us about them, but they don't do anything about them."

In other states, and at certain prisons in Connecticut, courts have ordered improvements. Alvin Bronstein, director of the American Civil Liberty Union's national prison project, has won more than 30 lawsuits for inmates nationwide.

If prisoners are not given safe and healthy shelter, they will return to the streets more violent, more prone to crime and more susceptible to illness than when they were locked up, he said.

"We claim to be a law-abiding democracy, and the law says we have to give {inmates} the minimum standards to live," Bronstein said. "Ninety percent of them will come back on the streets. I don't want these people coming out more dangerous, more angry, and worse than when they come in."

After this story was published, I discovered that Ventura had been sent into a segregated cell as silent punishment for his cooperation with our article. Feeling that transfer was dangerous damage to his future for a fair release date and possible adverse prison treatment, I contacted then U.S. Senator Chris Dodd and informed him of the circumstances.

As a result, the senator influenced Ventura's transfer to a New Hampshire corrections center. Thank goodness for him because Ventura informed me soon afterward that conditions there were reasonable.

But, later, Ventura re-contacted me through the mails to fiercely complain of his re-transfer to Cheshire. But, fortunately for Ventura and other inmates, the prison had been redesigned to better accommodate its heavy population.

Amazingly, before he was ultimately released, Ventura had spent time interacting through the mails to remarkably advance his education. He eventually earned his master's in religion while still behind bars.

"The administration would not allow me to have access to a typewriter, and both a 60,000- and 25,000-word thesis were hand written, and rewritten while sitting on the top bunk, legs hung over the side, and a banker box as a desk!'' said Ventura.

After his prison release he studied to receive his Doctor of Religious Education in March 2014. He became the leader of the Bible Believers Baptist Church of Imperial Beach, California. Next, he began working on a PhD. D. in World Religion. He became the Pastor the Bible Believer's Baptist Church Of Imperial Beach, California, the President of the Golden State Bible Baptist Prison Ministry and, President of the newly formed "Golden State Bible Baptist Institute

Most recently, Dr. Ventura completed "Haggai The Commentary" on the biblical book, Haggai of the Overview. During his work in the church, Dr. Ventura contacted me to urge my support of another inmate he knew.

After several years of my assistance with his writing skills, Efrain Pedro Morales, has been freed from prison and is now still working as a freelance writer while attempting to get another job to better support himself. But, unfortunately, he was rearrested while sleeping in his car and charged with drunken driving, a charge being contested in late 2019.

CHAPTER 11

INDIAN TRIBE OVERWHELMED BY CORRUPTION

Sometimes busy reporters, covering special beats focusing on government agencies, get tips about corrupt activities that they do not have the time to handle. One of The Courant's most experienced environmental reporters ever, Steve Grant, faced exactly that situation.

During his day to day work, Steve came across some inside sources who knew about irregularities within one of Connecticut's well known Indian tribe, The Schaghticokes, with ancient reservation grounds in Kent, Connecticut.

After some lengthy research and coordination among Steve, myself and our editors, I was assigned to investigate the curious situation, involving a deep tribal dispute.

The story, entitled Money Dispute Sours a Dream On Reservation, was published on May 10, 1986. After it appeared, it resulted in several angered members of the tribe suing me, The Courant and three of the Indians involved in cooperating with the newspaper's lengthy investigation for libel.

Below is the story relating to the failure of the lawsuit's plaintiffs to find any damages at all against myself, The Courant or the Indians who contributed their efforts to the investigation. That fictitious lawsuit became one of the most frustrating and fearsome experiences I have ever experienced in my life. Twice, the related tensions sent me to a small infirmary bed inside The Courant's first floor facilities for hours, to recover from the related stress.

Just before I prevailed, I will never, ever forget an episode in front of the courthouse, as I was standing during a recess after the jurors had begun deliberations. It was a beautiful, clear sunny day, but I was so tense awaiting the verdict that I had trouble appreciating it.

Suddenly, an elderly male juror walked closely near me, and with a smile, exclaimed, ''Good morning!'' I immediately looked up from the ground directly into his face and responded as he continued the walk into the courthouse. Then, almost immediately, I whispered to myself this exclamation: 'Don't even think about it!' In other words, I imagined he was signaling that I was about to be cleared.

Well…only minutes after I returned to court, the jury returned from its deliberations and cleared me. What a wondrous moment that was!

I was so incredibly relieved. An editor later asked me out to lunch to celebrate and discover the details of my experiences surrounding the trial of the lawsuit.

Here's The Courant's account of our wonderful win.

By Steven G. Vegh Courant Staff Writer

August 12, 1993

LITCHFIELD — A jury on Wednesday found The Courant did not libel four members of the Schaghticoke Indian tribe in a 1986 article that questioned how some tribe members spent federal and private funds.

The six-member jury did not explain its decision and was not obligated to. The jury deliberated about four hours after hearing testimony for three weeks and viewing at least 130 items entered as evidence.

"We felt all along that the suit was unjustified because we believed [the story] was truthful and that it was information that the public ought to know," said G. Claude Albert, the newspaper's deputy managing editor.

Harry Cohen, a New Milford lawyer who represented the plaintiffs, declined to comment on the jury's decision.

Gail Harrison, Edward Harrison, Alan Russell and Trudy Lamb Richmond sued the paper and reporter Thomas D. Williams on June 25, 1986, after Williams' article was published May 10, 1986.

The article questioned how certain tribe members spent $36,000 in private funds and $142,000 in federal funds given to the Schaghticokes between 1980 and 1983. The tribe maintains a 400-acre reservation in Kent.

The article also examined the handling of checks and vouchers by some tribe members and whether it was in keeping with tribal policies and funding agencies' rules.

The lawsuit claimed the article contained libelous statements "concerning the integrity, professional and occupational competency of the plaintiffs and their reputation for fair dealing."

The lawsuit additionally claimed that The Courant and Williams "meant by publishing said article that the plaintiffs were corrupt and had misallocated certain grant funding."

Ralph Elliot, the attorney for The Courant and Williams, said the crux of the case was the newspaper's motive in printing the article that named the four Schaghticokes.

"They were officers and officials of the Indian tribe," Elliot said. "They were, therefore, required to prove not only that the [portions of the article] were not substantially true, not only that they were defamatory, but also that when The Courant published them, it either knew they were not substantially true, or entertained serious doubts that they were true."

Williams said the jury decision vindicated the article, which he said described how federal and state agencies had not paid attention to complaints by some Schaghticokes about how other members were spending money received by the tribe.

"If that information can't get to the rest of the tribe through the news media, how is it going to get there?" Williams asked.

CHAPTER 12

TRASH HAULING BUSINESSES LINKED TO THE MAFIA

One of the toughest and scariest of investigative reporting efforts in my career occurred when Staff Reporter Daniel P. Jones, an environmental specialist and I probed for many months into the trash hauling industry.

Both Connecticut and nationally, trash company operators and officers have allegedly been involved with organized crime.

In two instances while working intensive back-to-back days on the subject, I was twice seriously threatened by two separate trash company operators. Nightmares followed, but there was nothing I could do about it. Complaining to authorities could create a conflict of interest that could halt our in-depth reporting which we knew would continue for story after story.

The Courant has not been alone in reporters' worries about interactions with hauler company operators.

The New York Times reported continuing concerns even years later when some trash officials faced investigations and allegations of corruption.

"A question: How many trash haulers exist in Connecticut? Ten? One hundred? A thousand?" asked The Times.

"Nobody knows for sure. Although the majority of the state's 169 municipalities do not provide garbage pickup for residents, forcing most people to hire private contractors, the industry is largely unregulated."

"The Legislature has refused for years to change the status quo, with unhappy results. For starters, a lack of state scrutiny allows trash haulers to keep the cost of garbage disposal high. More ominously, the absence of state oversight has made parts of the industry vulnerable to organized crime."

"There seems to be no doubt about the ties between the mob and the trash business in the minds of some legislators,"

See http://www.nytimes.com/2007/09/30/opinion/nyregionopinions/CT-trash.html

Right out of the Connecticut FBI comes a stirring report of the trash business' corruption led by a powerful leadership. A summary of it is here:

"He was dubbed the 'trash czar' by the media—James Galante, businessman and majority owner of 25 trash companies that controlled about 80 percent of the trash, or carting, industry in Connecticut and parts of eastern New York."

"But earlier this summer, Galante's reign ended when he pleaded guilty in federal court after a long-term multi-agency investigation of wrongdoing in the waste-hauling industry. Thirty-two others—including Galante's employees, his accountant, a silent partner with ties to New York organized crime, and a high-ranking member of the Genovese crime family—were also charged in the case and have all pleaded guilty."

"Galante was operating what's known as an illegal "property rights system"—when carting companies affiliated with organized crime groups assert they have a monopoly over certain 'stops,' or customer accounts (mostly commercial and municipal customers in this case). These companies collude with one another to divvy up the stops, fix prices, and rig contract bids. They also pay a so-called "mob tax" to keep their piece of the action."

"The result is a loss of competition and higher prices for customers. And woe to the carting companies that try to compete legally in this type of marketplace. They find trucks and other equipment vandalized, their employees threatened or assaulted by mob muscle, and their economic livelihood at stake." See Dirty Business Mob-Infested Trash Industry Cleaned Up.

SEE: ht HYPERLINK "https://archives.fbi.gov/archives/news/stories/2008/november/galante_110408"tps://archives.fbi.gov/archives/news/stories/2008/november/galante_11040 HYPERLINK "https://archives.fbi.gov/archives/news/stories/2008/november/galante_110408"8

So despite corruption in the state's trash businesses, which caused unnecessarily high disposal charges for state residents, little had been done up to July 2010 by law to prevent hauler corruption and price jacking.

"State law requires solid waste facilities and hazardous waste haulers to be licensed, but it does not require trash haulers to be licensed. Thus, trash haulers are not subject to the state agency oversight normally associated with licensees. But the Department of Environment (DEP) may issue stop orders to correct or abate violations of solid waste laws by anyone, including trash haulers," said Veronica Rose, Chief Legislative General Assembly Analyst. See https://www.cga.ct.gov/2010/rpt/2010-R-0309.htm

So, how about Dan Jones' and my experiences? We handled a dozen investigative stories on trash industry corruption a decade earlier. They revealed that the trash corruption beat seemingly never stops despite federal and state investigations. This is the critical focused series of three of our investigative articles on 'trashing it' in Connecticut.

AFTER A DECADE OF VIOLATIONS, DEP GETS TOUGH ON TRASH HAULER FIRST OF THREE PARTS: [STATEWIDE Edition]

DANIEL P. JONES and THOMAS D. WILLIAMS; Courant Staff Writers. Hartford Courant; Hartford, Conn. [Hartford, Conn]22 Aug 1996: A.1.

The state Department of Environmental Protection this month announced plans to deny a permit to a New York-based garbage hauler and his Connecticut business partner because of their record of "blatant, repeated violations of environmental statutes."

What the DEP didn't mention is that it has given the two haulers other permits for garbage facilities in recent years -- even though its files contained the same long history of dismal environmental compliance.

Experts say the decision could be a pivotal one that helps the DEP gain credibility as an enforcer of environmental rules.

The agency rejected Champion Recycling Industries Inc.'s application for a permit to build a trash-transfer station in West Haven. Champion's officers include Thomas Milo of Pelham, N.Y., and New Haven-area hauler Frank Perrotti. In June, Milo was indicted in White Plains, N.Y., on federal racketeering charges. He has pleaded not guilty.

A hearing officer's proposed decision to reject Milo's and Perrotti's application particularly singled out environmental violations by Perrotti's companies. The environmental records of the two haulers had not changed substantially between March 1995, when the DEP made a tentative decision to give the West Haven permit, and Aug. 9, when the DEP proposed denying it.

"I think it's a change in a policy that I see from DEP," said William R. Darcy, president of the Connecticut Resources Recovery Authority, which opposed the West Haven project. "I think it gives them greater credibility in terms of getting compliance."

Michele Sullivan, DEP spokeswoman, said the permits that Perrotti and Milo received in the past were granted based on reviews by the agency's waste bureau staff only. She said the latest decision followed a more rigorous process, which included an administrative hearing and a legal review because opponents of the proposed project intervened.

In recent years, Milo's and Perrotti's companies received a permit for a facility in Berlin, and a partnership in which Milo is involved received a permit in Danbury. At the time, their companies had racked up numerous violations of waste laws in their respective states, according to the DEP's files.

The Courant's review of the two haulers' records shows a history of environmental violations over a decade -- violations that largely were ignored by the DEP until the most recent decision.

The papers are part of the lengthy file on the application for the West Haven trash-transfer station -- submitted several years ago by Perrotti, Milo and a third partner under the name Champion Recycling Industries Inc. Perrotti is president; Milo is vice president.

The company was seeking to bring garbage from the Waterbury and New Haven areas to the trash-transfer station and take it to incinerators in Bridgeport and Lisbon. An internal DEP memo in the file says one of Perrotti's firms made "deliberately false statements" in a 1993 application for a Berlin recycling facility, for which it ultimately received state approval.

In one of the most serious environmental violations, a garbage hauling company owned by Milo, Suburban Carting Corp., dumped barrels of hazardous industrial waste into New York's Croton Point trash landfill in 1985. Such dumping was illegal, and Suburban paid a $5,000 fine, according to a New York document in the Connecticut DEP's files.

New York authorities fined Suburban Carting $500 in 1990 for violating a rule at a New Rochelle, N.Y., garbage transfer station; $3,000 in 1989 for transporting medical waste to a disallowed facility; and $100 in 1987 for spilling garbage onto the New York Thruway.

Champion Recycling Industries included those violations in its application.

Not reported, however, were problems and violations at the Al-Turi Landfill in Orange County, N.Y., which Milo co-owns. The dump has been polluting ground water off and on since 1980, according to New York Department of Environmental Conservation reports. The 100-acre landfill is on the banks of the Wallkill River and on top of a large aquifer, the principal water source for many local residents.

Despite the pollution and what a local watchdog group calls an "abhorrent record," New York officials recently renewed the landfill's permit but with many conditions listed in a 20-page report.

The report directed the landfill operator to stop hazardous leachate -- organic waste caused by groundwater or surface water's mixing with solid waste -- from continuing to contaminate ground water. In one month alone in 1995, the report said, there were 51 chemical readings in excess of the permit limits. The report said pollutants seeping out of the solid waste and ash landfill included arsenic, lead, chromium, benzene and vinyl chloride. The landfill operator was fined more than $1,000 last year and $2,500 this year for separate infractions involving unpermitted dumping of liquid waste and construction debris at the landfill.

The Courant made repeated attempts to talk with Milo and other officials at Suburban Carting. Greg Young, counsel for the company, declined to comment.

`Pattern' of violations

Perrotti had run-ins with Connecticut environmental inspectors beginning in 1986. That year, then-state Environmental Commissioner Stanley J. Pac rejected a permit application by Perrotti and said in the letter that waste facilities -- in Beacon Falls, North Haven and Branford -- in which Perrotti was involved had "a record of performance . . . which reveals a pattern and practice of repeated violation" of environmental laws and rules. Another DEP document says that Perrotti's company that operated in Beacon Falls, Salvage One Ltd., committed "very serious violations" there.

More recently, a trash-transfer station in New Haven, operated by DPL Refuse Inc., one of Perrotti's firms, was the subject of two notices of violation from the DEP. In 1991, Perrotti companies paid a $52,500 penalty for running a transfer station without a permit in Woodbridge, but Frank Perrotti & Sons Inc. and DPL Refuse Service did not admit to violating the law. The same internal DEP memo that alleged deliberate false statements were made also said Perrotti ran an illegal transfer station in Stratford, which was "a repeat of violations noted earlier in Woodbridge."

The memo was written in August 1993 by Thomas Pregman, a supervising environmental analyst in the DEP's waste, engineering and enforcement division. He recommended that the application for the Berlin recycling center be rejected, and that "the parties should be pursued for filing false information."

False statements

The DEP is required to verify the accuracy and truth of what is in an application. The application states that those who sign it must provide "true, accurate and complete information," and that "a false statement . . . may be punishable as a criminal offense" under state law.

The question that Pregman said was answered in a deliberately false manner on the application was a simple one.

The applicant -- Automated Salvage Transport Inc. -- was asked to list corporate officers. The names given were Frank Perrotti, president; Joseph Fiorillo, executive vice president, who is also vice president of Milo's Suburban Carting, and Edward Sayers Jr., secretary.

The next question was whether any of the parties involved had been associated with any other solid-waste facilities.

The answer, attested to by signatures from Automated Salvage's general manager, Dennis Soriano, and consultant Peter M. DeCarlo Jr., was "No."

"As you know that is not true," Pregman wrote in his memo. The parties involved have been associated with at least five waste facilities. Companies in the waste business for years, such as Perrotti's firms, are familiar with the application and its questions, according to the DEP.

"Whatever information I was given, that was in the application," said DeCarlo, the consultant. Asked if he had been supplied all the pertinent information, he said, "Of course not, or I would have included it."

Soriano said the misstatement was inadvertent and he noted that, despite the dispute, the DEP issued the permit.

Richard Barlow, chief of the DEP's Waste Management Bureau, gave Perrotti the permit for the Berlin facility in January 1994. Barlow says he had not been made aware deliberate misstatements allegedly had been made, and that by the time the application came before him, the issue had been resolved by his staff.

Sayers, executive vice president of DPL and secretary of Automated Salvage Transport, said the Perrotti companies "are extremely proud of our history of environmental compliance." Any violations the companies had were minor and corrected right away, he said.

The hearing officer who this month recommended that the West Haven project be denied saw it differently. Deborah Green said violations by Milo's and Perrotti's companies were the basis for her recommendation to deny the application.

"The compliance record from approximately 1992 to the present shows improvement over the dismal performance from approximately 1985 through 1991," Green wrote, "but still contains evidence of repeated violations."

A growing garbage empire

* A recent federal indictment and a proposed state DEP decision to deny a trash-transfer station permit in West Haven could slow the expansion into Connecticut of a New York garbage hauler who was identified 10 years ago in a New York State legislative report as having ties to organized crime.

Thomas Milo's business interests in Connecticut have included: Danbury: Milo's Suburban Carting Corp., of Mamaroneck, N.Y., one of 14 companies named in a recent federal indictment, owns part of Automated Waste Disposal in Danbury, which is the regional recycler for 10 Housatonic Valley towns: Kent, New Milford, Sherman, New Fairfield, Bridgewater, Brookfield, Danbury, Bethel, Newtown and Roxbury. The other part of AWD is owned by James Galante of New Fairfield, who was not named in the indictment.

Berlin: Milo was a part owner of Automated Material Handling, a private paper processor-recycler that also accepts plastic recyclables from the town of Bristol. A vice president of one of Milo's garbage hauling firms, Suburban Carting Corp., is now an officer of Automated Salvage Transport Inc., which received a state DEP permit in 1994 for a Berlin recycling center.

Enviro Express of Bridgeport, a subsidiary of Milo's Suburban Carting, hauls waste under contract with the Connecticut Resources

Recovery Authority-financed trash-to-energy plant in Bridgeport, which serves 14 towns. The contract is with the plant's builder-operator, Wheelabrator Technologies Inc.

Portland: Perrotti and Joseph Fiorillo, vice president of Suburban Carting, are among the officers of Automated Salvage Transport Inc., which is seeking a contract to run a trash-transfer station in town.

West Haven: Milo and Frank Perrotti, a New Haven-area garbage hauler, are applicants for a state DEP permit for a trash-transfer station, under the company name of Champion Recycling Industries Inc. This month the DEP issued a proposed decision to deny the application.

STATE AGENCIES FALL SHORT IN DEALING WITH OUT OF STATE TRASH HAULERS SECOND OF THREE PARTS: [STATEWIDE Edition]

THOMAS D. WILLIAMS and DANIEL P. JONES; Courant Staff Writers. Hartford Courant; Hartford, Conn. [Hartford, Conn]23 Aug 1996: A.1.

Five years ago, when the state's big trash-to-energy plant in Hartford wasn't getting enough waste from area towns, managers came up with what seemed like a good idea: invite in garbage haulers from New York.

The program was to save the more than 50 towns paying the plant's bills millions of dollars, because the plant would consume trash it got paid for, instead of having to burn costly coal.

But critics say officials at the Connecticut Resources Recovery Authority and the state Department of Environmental Protection have sometimes turned a blind eye to checkered backgrounds of some of the companies and, in the process, allowed those haulers to gain a regrettable presence in Connecticut's garbage industry.

Connecticut has no specific laws that prevent haulers who face criminal charges -- or even those convicted of anti-competitive behavior -- from obtaining trash permits from the DEP or from dumping trash at state-operated trash facilities.

Seven haulers dumped more than 171,000 tons of out-of-state garbage at the Hartford plant in the 1996 fiscal year alone, according to the trash authority.

One of the haulers, Delmar Waste Services Ltd., faces state criminal charges in New York involving a Mafia-related scheme to drive out competitors and increase garbage- collection prices in Manhattan. Delmar is accused of being part of a cartel that used threats and violence, including attempted murder, assault and arson, to bully competitors out of business and keep prices artificially high. Delmar Waste Services Ltd., Delmar Recycling Corp. and Patrick Pecoraro, their owner, have pleaded not guilty.

And the operator of a Danbury trash-transfer station that receives garbage from New York and sends it to Hartford, is in business in another venture with Thomas Milo, of Pelham, N.Y. Milo faces federal criminal charges that he was part of a Mafia cartel that used arson, bribery and violence to dominate the garbage-hauling industry in suburbs north of New York City and parts of southwestern Connecticut. He has pleaded not guilty.

"The recent indictments raise very direct and, unavoidably, some profound and important issues about the state dealing with companies that may not have the integrity and the ability that we want, and perhaps demand, as a condition of working for the state," said state Attorney General Richard Blumenthal.

Bob Gross of West Hartford, a former recycling and trash company owner and a veteran observer of the region's waste industry, said there is "no question there's price- fixing going on" in Connecticut and elsewhere in the industry.

Because towns and businesses often are afraid of garbage haulers, they rarely complain that they're being gouged, Gross said.

Connecticut residents pay trash- disposal fees either in taxes through their town's garbage-hauling contract or through direct assessment by haulers, and they indirectly pay for trash-disposal at virtually any business they patronize in higher prices of products or services.

Those are the people who really are hurt by price fixing in the garbage industry, Gross said, and they don't even know it's happening.

Minimal review

The Connecticut Resources Recovery Authority says it does not check whether any of the out-of- state haulers it deals with have been convicted of or charged with criminal violations -- including violations related to the industry, such as anti-competitive activities, extortion or bid-rigging.

Paul Guidone, executive vice president of the authority, said the agency also does not check whether out-of-state haulers have committed environmental violations, such as illegally dumping hazardous or medical waste. The authority reviews the financial backgrounds of the companies, he said, and makes a note of any environmental violations that might come to its attention.

The trash authority manages the operations at the incinerators where the haulers dump garbage, and the DEP issues permits for trash-transfer stations, landfills, incinerators and recycling plants.

At the DEP, officials who enforce solid-waste rules say state law allows them to consider applicants' backgrounds for environmental violations only -- not criminal histories.

Three years ago, the trash authority's president, William R. Darcy, said he was concerned about moves into the state by trash haulers and landfill operators who were believed to have ties to organized crime. At the time, the authority was fighting an application by Milo and a partner for a DEP permit to build a trash-transfer station in Danbury, which ultimately was built.

A 1986 report from a New York Assembly committee chaired by Democratic New York Assemblyman Maurice Hinchey, who now serves in Congress, linked Milo to the Genovese crime family.

Darcy urged Connecticut lawmakers to strengthen a law that allows the DEP to investigate the backgrounds of individuals and companies seeking solid-waste permits. But the proposed changes were never adopted.

So the trash authority has continued to do business with companies that have questionable records. Darcy said the agency would be sued if it ceased to do business with companies that merely have been indicted, not convicted.

Underground ties

Many in the industry fear that allowing some of New York's haulers into Connecticut has opened the door to problems.

Aside from environmental concerns about added air pollution and traffic congestion caused by the longer trucking hauls, Connecticut firms could be in danger of being pushed out of the market, leading to higher trash-collection costs.

Milo was among seven men indicted in June by a federal grand jury in White Plains, N.Y., on mob-related racketeering, extortion and tax conspiracy charges. Milo and the other defendants in the case all have pleaded not guilty and are awaiting trial. Greg Young, counsel for Milo's company, declined to comment.

In the 61-count indictment, prosecutors say a Mafia-controlled cartel used arson, bribery and violence to dominate the garbage-hauling industry in the suburbs north of New York, allowing companies to "grossly inflate" the price of garbage collection.

Milo's ties to haulers doing business in Connecticut are extensive. Milo and James E. Galante are officers of Automated Waste Disposal Inc. in Danbury. Galante also operates Transfer Systems Inc. of Danbury, which hauls New York trash to the Hartford incinerator. Galante's office in Danbury referred questions to a Danbury attorney and secretary of Transfer Systems, Jack Garamella, who did not return calls.

One of Milo's companies named in the federal indictment is Suburban Carting of Mamaroneck, N.Y. The company's chief financial officer, Carmine Mascia, serves as treasurer and assistant secretary of Transfer Systems.

Suburban Carting and Enviro Express, another of Milo's companies named in the federal indictment, have gained a major share of the garbage-hauling business in Connecticut's Fairfield County. Enviro Express hauls garbage from more than a dozen Connecticut towns to a state-financed incinerator in Bridgeport.

Earlier this month, in a proposed decision by a DEP hearing officer, Milo and Frank Perrotti, a New Haven-area trash entrepreneur, were turned down for a state permit for a trash-transfer station in West Haven because of dismal records in complying with environmental laws. A final decision is pending and could be challenged in court.

STATE LACKS LAW REQUIRING BACKGROUND CHECKS FOR TRASH HAULERS LAST OF THREE PARTS: [STATEWIDE Edition]

THOMAS D. WILLIAMS and DANIEL P. JONES; Courant Staff Writers. Hartford Courant; Hartford, Conn. [Hartford, Conn]24 Aug 1996: A.1.

Portland's selectmen were on the verge of turning over their recycling and trash-transfer station to a large New Haven waste hauler in June when the news hit.

The hauler's partner in another project had been charged in New York with conspiring with other waste companies and using violence to drive competitors out of the market.

The selectmen had wanted to accept what seemed like a fantastic deal for Portland. But they were unsure about the extent of the hauler's involvement with his indicted partner. The selectmen, who temporarily rescinded their approval of the contract with Automated Salvage Transport Inc., now are trying to decide what to do next.

First Selectman Edward L. Kalinowski said the 61-count federal indictment of Thomas Milo of New York and his company, Suburban Carting Corp., was so serious that town leaders felt they had to look into his relationship with Automated's owner, Frank Perrotti.

Perrotti said the contract should be judged on its merits, not on his relationship "with a man who has not been convicted of any crime."

Kalinowski said that because the trash industry has such a stigma to it, "I would favor some sort of background checks {on trash haulers} as long it doesn't invade a person's privacy," said Kalinowski. "But, the question is, do you have the time in a small town like this to conduct an inquiry? Would you have the police do it?"

An increased presence

During the past five years, garbage haulers that have been indicted in New York for anti-competitive practices and acts of violence have stepped up their presence in Connecticut. Every day they haul tons of garbage from New York to Connecticut's trash-transfer stations and incinerators.

In New York, control of the garbage industry by cartels of haulers tied to organized crime has caused broad concern among public officials and, according to two pending indictments there, cost businesses and residents millions of dollars a year.

But in Connecticut, as Portland's board of selectmen learned, there is little regulation at any level.

Officials at the state Department of Environmental Protection say no specific law prevents trash haulers indicted or even convicted of anti-competitive behavior from obtaining trash permits from the DEP or doing business with the Connecticut Resources Recovery Authority.

"We don't control the haulers," said Richard Barlow, chief of the bureau of waste management at the state DEP. "We don't regulate them. . . . The way I read the existing statute we would have no way of taking that into account. (The DEP's responsibility) applies only to environmental violations, not extortion."

The Connecticut Resources Recovery Authority has called for legislation requiring background checks of individuals and companies that want permits to dump or haul trash in the state. The laws never passed, and CRRA President William R. Darcy says the trash authority has little choice but to continue to do business with companies under indictment.

Who is checking?

Close to 150 trash haulers advertise in Connecticut's "Business-to-Business" telephone book for the state's 169 towns.

The state police and the FBI both say they rely on investigators with knowledge of organized crime to handle inquiries about the trash industry, but only as a side duty.

However, a state police detective with considerable knowledge about the industry was reassigned to other duties six years ago. The FBI agent who extensively investigated Connecticut trash haulers during the 1980s retired three years ago.

"{Haulers} should be required to have renewable licenses, just like drivers do," the retired FBI agent, Daniel C. Mahan, said in a recent interview. "They should provide the state with complete background records on their company."

An FBI inquiry of the trash industry in the 1980s found that eight haulers based in and around Greater Hartford were cheating state businesses, raising prices by as much as 128 percent in one year. Between early 1985 and May 1987, when these haulers were overcharging their customers, they made $51 million, the FBI said.

The haulers were acquitted because federal prosecutors did not prove the activities affected commerce between Connecticut and another state.

State Attorney General Richard Blumenthal later sued the same group of haulers for state anti-trust violations and won $1 million in damages for the towns involved.

"The {waste-disposal} industry has a long and regrettable record of criminal infiltration and legal violations, including anti-trust and connections to organized crime," Blumenthal said. "You ought to be able to consider any facts affecting the integrity or ability of the company in connection with its performance."

`The safest course," Blumenthal added, "would be to require it by statute" to avoid lawsuits by garbage companies.

Dennis Soriano, general manager of Automated Salvage Transport of Berlin, said he does not think background checks are needed.

`I don't know why the waste industry would be singled out," said Soriano, whose company is owned by Perrotti.

Michele Sullivan, the DEP's spokeswoman, said the agency generally supports broadening the state's ability to conduct background checks of applicants. She said the state is exploring whether such changes could be made administratively, without seeking new legislation. If changes in the law are needed, she said, the agency will support them in the next General Assembly.

Nuala Forde, Gov. John G. Rowland's spokeswoman, said the administration will seriously consider proposing new legislation if it is needed.

A warning from New York

Connecticut should be cautious about dealing with companies that have ties to organized crime, even those that are indicted but not yet convicted, said Rep. Maurice D. Hinchey, D-N.Y.

"By doing business with them, you are . . . facilitating their ability to carry on their illegal or illicit activities," he said.

Hinchey also warned that toxic waste often is mixed illegally with conventional waste, thereby saving the hauler "the large amounts of money it costs to get rid of toxic wastes legitimately."

Ten years ago, when the congressman was a New York state legislator, he was chairman of an Assembly committee that detailed the Mafia's involvement in New York's waste industry in a lengthy report. While working on the report, Hinchey said, he was threatened and offered money to back off. "And that was not the worst of it," he said. "The indifference we received from some of the authorities was worse than the threats of physical violence and offers of bribes."

Hinchey's report inspired no real change in New York law. But for a while it did get some attention in Connecticut.

Milo, one of the haulers indicted in New York in June, was identified in Hinchey's report as having suspected ties to organized crime.

In June 1988, news stories revealed that officials with the Connecticut attorney general's office and the state trash authority were aware of the conclusions in Hinchey's report. Nonetheless, the Connecticut Resources Recovery Authority approved a contract to allow Milo's company, Suburban Carting, to haul trash from a Fairfield transfer station to the trash-to-energy plant in Bridgeport.

Sen. Joseph I. Lieberman, D-Conn., who was then state attorney general, proposed a law similar to New Jersey's, which would give the attorney general and environmental officials broad powers to scrutinize waste haulers' backgrounds before granting them trash permits.

The recommendation was whittled down into today's law that requires the state DEP to consider the environmental records of waste industry operators before granting them permits for landfills, incinerators or trash-transfer stations.

Lieberman said he still believes trash haulers should be required to file extensive reports on their histories.

Soon after this trash hauler series ended, we started a probe of the industries' irregularities.

Here it is!

Officials Press For Probe Of Trash Hauling Giant

By DANIEL P. JONES And THOMAS D. WILLIAMS; Courant Staff Writers Hartford Courant [Hartford, Conn] 29 Aug 1999: B1.

Ten towns in northeastern Connecticut, citing drastic price increases and scant competition among garbage haulers, want the state attorney general to investigate industry giant Waste Management Inc.

As a result of the rising costs, "towns in the northeast will see holes in their budgets" next year, said John E. Burke Jr., Killingly's town council chairman and chairman of the Northeastern Connecticut Council of Governments.

In a recent council vote, elected leaders of the 10 towns unanimously adopted a resolution requesting the investigation "in light of recent price increases . . . and the diminishment of marketplace choice . . . as a result of recent acquisitions by Waste Management."

Price increases for garbage hauling and disposal could force some towns to raise taxes or reduce services.

Waste Management, the nation's largest hauling and disposal company, denies it has stifled competition and says it won contracts with at least three of the towns -- including Woodstock and Thompson -- through competitive bidding.

"We're certainly not concerned about any inquiry in this regard," said Dennis C. Vacco, a Waste Management vice president of governmental affairs.

Attorney General Richard Blumenthal, meanwhile, said his office already had begun an investigation of the trash-hauling and waste industry statewide, based on complaints alleging illegal, anti-competitive practices. He said it began weeks ago, before his office heard about the resolution.

"We're concerned about Waste Management Inc., but our investigation is not limited to that company," Blumenthal said. He said he wants to determine whether there has been collusion or conspiracy to allocate territories and fix prices.

Texas-based Waste Management has long been in the waste-disposal business in Connecticut. But in recent months the company has become a dominant player in the hauling end of the business, by acquiring a group of firms that collectively served about half the state. Waste Management also owns two of the six trash incinerators in the state and runs a regional landfill for the ash residue from incinerators.

The company recently acquired several hauling firms from Frank Perrotti Jr., a Woodbridge-based hauler who was a major industry player, particularly in central Connecticut. Waste Management also bought Yaworski Trucking of Canterbury, a company that had a sizable share of the hauling market in the northeastern part of the state.

Northeast Waste Systems, which was among the former Perrotti firms acquired by Waste Management, told customers in northeastern Connecticut in April that the price for waste hauling and disposal would increase by about 20 percent on May 1.

Waste Management is the parent firm of Wheelabrator Technologies Co., which owns and operates a garbage incinerator in Lisbon. The Lisbon plant told its customers in February that the per-ton fee to unload trash there would jump in March to $75, up from $53.

Garbage hauling and disposal costs, although not a subject people usually talk about, affect every household and every business. When they increase, they are passed on to homeowners, taxpayers, business owners and consumers.

In northeastern Connecticut, a paucity of bidders for hauling and disposal contracts has put Woodstock and Thompson in what elected leaders say is a budgetary noose. They say that last spring they sent invitations to bid to more than two dozen companies but received only one bid that covered all the services requested.

The only such bid Thompson received was from the company that had its last contract, Yaworski Trucking, one of the firms purchased by Waste Management. Woodstock found itself in a similar situation, when Yaworski was the only bidder to submit a price list for all recyclables.

In each case, the rival bidder was Browning-Ferris Industries, Waste Management's chief competitor nationally. BFI previously had Woodstock's contract. In the latest round of bids in Woodstock, both companies offered prices that were triple what the town had been paying.

Willimantic Waste Paper, one of the few surviving small companies in eastern Connecticut, submitted a bid in Thompson, but only for recyclables, not garbage. Tim DeVivo, one of Willimantic Waste's officers, said he is trying to compete against Waste Management in a new garbage-hauling venture. But he said he simply doesn't have the trucks to bid for contracts in many towns.

"Small haulers are the lifeblood of the business," he said. "But when they've all been bought out, that leaves little competition."

Blumenthal's inquiry and the displeasure of northeastern Connecticut officials might be the least of Waste Management's concerns.

Earlier this month in a filing with securities regulators, the company said the U.S. Justice Department was looking into its Massachusetts operations to determine whether it engaged in illegal restraint of trade or anti-competitive acquisitions of waste disposal and hauling businesses.

In the same filing, Waste Management said the U.S. Securities and Exchange Commission and the New York Stock Exchange were looking into multi-million-dollar sales of stock by insiders prior to a July 6 company announcement that warned of lower projected profits. The warning triggered a sharp decline in the company's stock price.

Here is a typical in-depth piece elsewhere on the corrupt mob influence within the garbage hauling business and its sometimes clean up.

Dirty Business Mob-Infested Trash Industry Cleaned Up

SEE:
https://www.gloucestercitynews.net/clearysnotebook/2008/11/dirty-business.html

Dan Jones and I did scores of stories together on the trash industry, largely because Dan specialized in environmental concerns impacted by controversial local, state and federal investigations, while I focused upon sloppy governmental probes and activities. But once in a while, I became fascinated with features on nature.

CHAPTER 13

WILD BIRDS ARE MY ALL-TIME FAVORITE CREATURES

As a reporter and a bird lover for almost all of my life, I can never, ever forget a chance episode while I was working as a state court reporter which spontaneously drew me into writing my most joyous news story feature ever.

Ever since I was a boy, living in a 1700s salt box just hundreds of yards down Duck Pond Road from my well-known ornithologist Uncle Dillon Ripley's pond loaded with captured, well taken care of ducks, I have been fascinated with birds of all varieties.

In fact as a teenager, during the record floods of 1955 from back-to-back hurricanes, I helped his sister-in-law, my Aunt Dottie Ripley, save ducks. At the time of the crisis, we were working without Uncle Dillon because he was then in New Haven and not immediately aware of the pond's crisis. Ducks were floating free out of the broken, fenced in pond and down Butternut Brook for close to a half mile. In and out of the shallowest, rushing brook water Aunt Dottie and I, as best we could, propped up fencing and waded with nets readied for those difficult duck captures.

Here's how Uncle Dillon described the situation in his wondrous book, A Paddling of Ducks.

"Then there are the acts of God...The floods following, Hurricane Diane came upon us all unwitting In a night of rain. This following a whole day and a half of rain, our little brook, swollen beyond all comprehension, overran its banks in a way that had perhaps not happened since they were first gouged out in some convulsion of the dwindling post glacier stream a few thousand years ago. Certainly, there was no evidence to indicate that our brook had ever overflowed its banks or been so swollen in recent history."

At one point, when back inside the screened pond after our river snares, I recall my attempt to capture small Dama wallaby, related to kangaroos. As I, snuck, bent over, and cornered it next to fencing, that wallaby jumped right over my head and back and ran away! I was astonished beyond belief! Today I remember this startling episode as if it just happened!

So here I now was, four and a half decades later as a news reporter covering Hartford Superior Court one day, when instead of a so called 'legal eagle' court story flying to mind, a fascinating and genuine nature wild bird tale flourished right alongside that very court! As it turned out, two hawks were nesting right on top of an eagle sculpture carved into the side of the courthouse!

Here is that very story.

HANGIN' WITH THE HAWKS A HARTFORD SAGA OF LIFE AND DEATH: [7 SPORTS FINAL Edition]

By Thomas D. Williams and Bob MacDonnell

Hartford Courant [Hartford, Conn] 09 July 2000: H1.

The spectacle -- the birth of two chicks over Easter weekend, the death of their mother a week later and the father hawk raising the fledglings alone -- has captured the attention of court clerks, jurors, uniformed sheriffs, lawyers in business suits and neighborhood residents all spring.

Daily, dozens of people gathered along Washington Street, craning their necks for views of the hawks nesting on an eagle sculpture at the civil court. Some bring cameras while others train binoculars on the birds.

Late last month, the fledglings began flying in and out of the nest, sometimes disappearing for minutes and hours at a time. The nest is vacant now. A sheriff recently saw one of the youngsters fall off a park tree branch next to the court, hit the ground and flap around until airborne again. Some regular onlookers are feeling like sad empty nesters.

"My God, I feel like my kid is going off to college," said Brenda Pierscinski, a court clerk.

On the third floor in the adjacent Lafayette Street criminal court, court stenographers set up a small telescope for employees to watch the hawk soap opera. One said she is looking for a photo of one of the hawks so she can create "hawking justice" T-shirts for the "legal eagles" in the courthouse.

"In a crazy sort of way, it brings people together," Elaine Halloran, a veteran criminal court clerk, said. "People keep asking one another: `What are they doing today?' "

The hawks began building the bulky nest in February, and their courtship rituals, including flight displays and piercing screams, quickly drew much attention. By late March, the female had laid eggs and was incubating them, along with the male. They hunted in the court's adjacent small park and beyond, periodically returning to the nest with food for their two youngsters.

Soon after the chicks hatched, the female hawk was injured when it struck a tree or building while being harassed by crows. Barbara Chappell, a court administrative assistant, found the injured bird on the ground. She called a wildlife rehabilitator to care for it, but the hawk died the next day.

The male hawk was left to fend for the chicks -- tiny white balls of down barely a week old. Crows, natural enemies of raptors, harassed him, sometimes making it difficult for him to stray from the nest to hunt.

Hawk-watchers became concerned, especially after construction workers, using a huge noisy crane, began repairing and tarring the roof directly above the nest. Court personnel concerned about the construction disruption placed at least a half dozen calls to the state Department of Environmental Protection, the Audubon Society and other organizations seeking advice.

Worried the chicks would not survive without their mother amid all the nearby street traffic and other city dangers, some observers asked whether the DEP could provide food for the hawks or remove the chicks from the nest and raise them in captivity.

"We thought Dad would do fine and it was best not to intervene, and that proved wise," said Chris Vann, a biologist for the DEP Wildlife Division.

The male hawk constantly perched on the top southeast corner of an abandoned, nearby 14-story office building to seek out prey in the small court-side park below while also glancing down at the nesting chicks.

"There are a lot of human fathers who could learn a lot from him," Halloran said. "He's quite a hawk. When the crows came to dive at him, he just stayed there, regally, without a move."

In mid-June, the larger of the two fledglings, a female, hopped off the nest to an adjacent ledge. Late in the afternoon, a gust of wind caught the young bird, knocking it from the ledge. It floated 30 or 40 feet and landed on a judge's black Suburban. It hooked a claw in the car's back door hinge, but someone freed it and it continued hopping along the car's roof.

Soon a dispute broke out between several court employees after two of them used an article of clothing to move the bird to a tree next to traffic-laden Washington Street.

Clerk Holly Scalzo, who has been closely monitoring the hawks for months, yelled at the two to leave the bird alone. "I can't take this anymore. It's getting to be too much," she said.

Chris Vann was called and chased the bird a short distance along the street before capturing it and returning it to the nest. He said the bird was uninjured but predicted it might happen again. The birds did from time to time jump from the nest to the roof, but were always able to return to the nest.

"It's touch and go. A lot of young birds get themselves into trouble. This is a difficult time for them," Vann said.

Red-tailed hawks are the most common and adaptable raptors in Connecticut. Although they usually nest in wooded areas near open fields, they will adapt to various nesting habitats, even in urban settings, to try to catch rats, mice, squirrels, pigeons and other birds.

Hartford residents Richard Hernandez and Marsha Banas have appreciated the sight of hawks in the city. They used to check on the chicks with their binoculars while walking along Washington Street.

"We live in the neighborhood and came by every day to check their progress," Hernandez said. "It's something you don't normally see in the city. It's great for Hartford."

HERE ARE TWO OF BOB MACDONNELL'S BEAUTIFUL PHOTOS OF THOSE RED-TAILED HAWKS NESTING ON THE HARTFORD SUPERIOR COURT'S EXPRESSIONISTIC EAGLE SCULPTURE. THE LOYAL PAPA SAVED HIS BABIES LIVES AFTER HIS WIFE DIED WHEN STRIKING EITHER A TREE OR THE SUPREME COURT BUILDING WHILE SOMETIMES BEING WATCHED BY CROWS NEARBY.

Illustrations in the COURANT STORY---THE PHOTOS By Bob MacDonnell

Dozens of people joined the hawk-watch every day on Washington Street. The papa hawk was harassed by a crow as it was around its nest on the Superior Court building on Washington Street.

Crows repeatedly mobbed the male in flight after the female hawk died and threatened the nest when the male was away. The two fledglings were raised by the male hawk alone after the female flew into the side of a building or tree while being chased by those crows and died.

Crows feel threatened by hawks and sometimes sense those big wingers might find and kill their black-winged babies. The Papa red-tailed hawk, left, fed his fledgling chicks in their nest built on that statue of an eagle on the Superior Court building in Hartford. The chicks' mother died a week after they hatched, and the male then fed and raised them by himself.

Here is the absolutely scariest of bird stories I have ever read, written by Carl Zimmer New York Times Staff Repoter on Sept. 19, 2019

"The number of birds in the United States and Canada has declined by 3 billion, or 29 percent, over the past half-century, scientists find. The skies are emptying out.

The number of birds in the United States and Canada has fallen by 29 percent since 1970, scientists reported on Thursday. There are 2.9 billion fewer birds taking wing now than there were 50 years ago.

The analysis, published in the journal Science, is the most exhaustive and ambitious attempt yet to learn what is happening to avian populations. The results have shocked researchers and conservation organizations.

In a statement in January 2020, David Yarnold, president and chief executive of the National Audubon Society, called the findings "a full-blown crisis." Experts have long known that some bird species have become vulnerable to extinction. But the new study, based on a broad survey of more than 500 species, reveals steep losses even among such traditionally abundant birds as robins and sparrows.

There are likely many causes, the most impactful of which is the great harm caused by pesticides starting as far back as the 1960s. This next story describes well a world that is losing its birds:

https://www.nytimes.com/2019/09/19/science/bird-populations-america-canada.html

CHAPTER 14

THE GULF WAR

Beyond such fun feature stories, one of my most intense investigations during my almost four decades at The Courant became the sad and mentally disturbing topic involving Gulf War illnesses. It seemed once I started writing about the topic I could never stop. I wrote about the subject off and on for over a decade.

Below the brief summary descriptions of the conflicts are two of my stories showing how, over time, the Gulf War has continued to haunt the Pentagon, The U.S. Department of Veterans Affairs, caring for sick troops and the families of those serving the Army, Navy, Marine and Air Force veterans.

Summaries Gulf War

The Gulf War broke out twice. The lead up to the first war began with the Iraqi invasion of Kuwait in August 1990. It was met with immediate economic sanctions by the United Nations against Iraq. The battle following involved a U.S.-led coalition, including 34 nations. It started in August 1990 and ended in February 1991.

"After 42 days of relentless attacks by the allied coalition in the air and on the ground, U.S. President George H.W. Bush declared a cease-fire on February 28; by that time, most Iraqi forces in Kuwait had either surrendered or fled," says this lengthy war history on the Internet. SEE: www.history.com/topics/persian-gulf-war.

The second phase, starting in March 2003 and ending in December 2011, was caused when U.S. President George W. Bush " without further U.N. approval, issued an ultimatum on March 17, 2003. (It demanded) that Saddam Hussein step down from power and leave Iraq within 48 hours, under threat of war. Hussein refused, and the second Persian Gulf War–more generally known as the Iraq War–began three days later," SEE: www.history.com

Now, one after the other, are two crucial stories about the tremendously adverse and tragic tortuous impact of the war's pollutants on thousands of U.S. service members from all branches of the military.

Gulf War Illnesses Real

By Thomas D. Williams, Staff Reporter Hartford Courant

Brain scans of some Persian Gulf War soldiers show damage by exposure to wartime chemicals, a new Pentagon-sponsored study reveals.

The study, combined with earlier related studies, contradict claims by the Pentagon since the Gulf War that low-level chemical agents were not common on battlefields, or, if they were evident, that they could not have been seriously harmful to veterans.

Many veterans have complained of persistent illnesses in the years since the war.

"It basically penetrates the denials that they were not sick from Gulf War-related exposures," said Dr. James L. Fleckenstein, a professor of radiology at the University of Texas and one of those responsible for the study. "Now we can move from a point when Gulf War Syndrome was debated, to a time when Gulf War disease can be diagnosed, and hopefully an effective treatment can be developed."

"It confirms what we have known for a long time, that there were serious exposures to chemical warfare out there in the battlefields," said former U.S. Sen. Donald W. Riegle Jr., a Michigan Democrat.

As chairman of a Senate committee, it was Riegle who first gathered evidence in 1993 and 1994 that Gulf War soldiers had been exposed to chemical warfare. The evidence revealed in part that hundreds of thousands of chemical alarms had sounded after winds carried chemicals over battlefields during allied bombings of Iraqi chemical weapons plants.

More than 100,000 of the 690,000 Gulf War veterans who served at the height of the 1990-91 war, have reported suffering from symptoms such as memory loss, loss of balance, sleep disorders, depression, exhaustion, joint pain, diarrhea and problems with concentration.

These symptoms, the studies say, are consistent with veterans' exposures to chemicals, including chemical warfare, anti-chemical warfare drugs and pesticides.

A group of Navy Seabees as well as some Army soldiers took special magnetic resonance brain scans, which showed they have 10 percent to 25 percent lower levels of a certain chemical in the brain stem and gray matter than healthy soldier-subjects, the new study shows.

The brain stem controls some of the body's reflexes, and the gray matter controls movement, memory and emotion. A total of 46 service people were studied. The collection of data took three to four months and was completed in September 1998.

"The Department of Defense is always interested in high quality research that provides us information concerning the complex set of health problems being encountered by our Persian Gulf War veterans," said James Turner, a Pentagon spokesman.

"'We look forward to seeing the work in a peer-reviewed scientific journal of stature. Until then, it would be inappropriate for the [department] to comment on an unreleased research paper we haven't seen."

He said the defense department is continuing to care for active duty Gulf War veterans experiencing problems they believe are associated with their service during the war.

So far, Turner said, the department has provided special physical exams for 38,135 veterans and some family members.

Last month, a report from the Rand Corp., also funded by the Pentagon, revealed that the use of the drug pyridostigmine bromide (PB) by 250,000 soldiers during the Persian Gulf War "cannot be ruled out" as a cause of lingering illnesses in some veterans.

The PB pills were supplied to service members by the military despite the experimental nature of their use, and despite the fact that they were effective only against soman nerve gas and dangerous to use in the face of potential sarin gas, accessible to the Iraqis.

Fleckenstein and Dr. Robert Haley, an associate professor of internal medicine and chief of epidemiology, both working at the University of Texas Southwestern Medical Center in Dallas were in charge of the brain scan study.

It is a significant follow up to earlier studies by Haley of Gulf War veterans and was funded by the U.S. Department of Defense and the [Ross] Perot Foundation of Dallas.

Haley said the findings were significant not only because they show the veterans were telling the truth about their exposure to chemical warfare, but because their brain injuries may be treatable.

He said brain cells are not missing in the patients examined, just damaged or atrophied. Although there is no known treatment as of yet, Haley added, there is medical research underway to regenerate nerve cells.

"Some of these [veterans] are profoundly disabled, [some] barely able to drive to the store," Fleckenstein said. "The findings suggest a substantial loss of brain cells in the areas that could explain the veterans' symptoms."

The results were released in a press conference Tuesday at the 85th Scientific Assembly of the Radiological Society of North America.

Twenty-two sick Gulf War U.S. Navy veterans studied had lower levels of certain chemicals in the brain than was detected in 18 healthy veterans. That study was consistent with a second one of six Gulf War Army veterans. The doctors doing the study were not told which veterans were healthy or which had symptoms of illness, Haley and Fleckenstein said.

In earlier research, Haley said, he and Texas research doctors identified three primary symptoms indicating brain impairment in sick Gulf War veterans.

Their disabilities were consistent with the soldiers' exposures to chemical nerve gas, side effects from PB tablets and insect repellents, and pesticides used in soldiers' flea collars, the earlier study said.

Critics of the Pentagon quickly reacted to the new study. "Why is Dr. Haley able to figure this out when our government friends and their scientists were unable to do so for so long?" asked retired U.S. Army Maj. Barry Kapplan of Union.

Kapplan, a Gulf War veteran, spent tens of thousands of dollars trying to cure a variety of illnesses he and family members contracted and which he believes were related to his war exposures.

He said: "It's nine years late and a whole bunch of medical bills short,'" he said. "What is this going to do for the veterans now? It's so long after the Gulf War, it's hard to believe veterans can still be treated."

Riegle, the former senator, now working for an international public relations firm whose work includes health-related issues, called the new study a "chilling and persuasive finding."

"It demonstrates again that the Pentagon has worked hardest not to get to the full truth. And, we have all those walking wounded who need medical help and compensation, and they are not getting it," Riegle explained. "These findings lend new urgency to bring this issue back to the forefront. I think the president has an obligation to act as the commander in chief, if the Pentagon doesn't do so."

This tragic war story of continuously and mysteriously ill veterans continued endlessly resulting in basic down to earth mental torcher and deaths. The wars were over, but the government and often veterans' paid medical battles never ended.

GULF WAR'S VEIL OF VICTORY A DECADE AFTER ROUTING IRAQ: VETERANS PLAGUED BY ILLNESS; MILITARY BRILLIANCE LOSES LUSTER: [7 SPORTS FINAL 17 Jan 2001

By Matthew Hay Brown and Thomas D. Williams Courant Staff Writers

Ten years ago, this morning, eight U.S. Army Apache helicopters stole low across the Saudi desert toward Iraq. Their targets: a pair of radar bases, 20 miles apart, along Iraq's western border.

The choppers struck at 2:38 a.m. Baghdad time, launching a storm of Hellfire missiles to level the isolated outposts. In the hours before dawn, wave after wave would flow through the breach, stinging military bases, communications centers, power plants and other targets.

The 1991 Persian Gulf War had begun.

Images of the conflict endure: U.S. Patriot missiles knocking incoming Iraqi Scuds out of the sky. Precision-guided munitions homing in on military targets. Dazed Iraqi soldiers crawling over sand dunes to surrender to their American counterparts. President

Bush beaming from the reviewing stand as gulf war veterans marched past in the Washington, D.C., victory parade.

At the end of the Cold War and the beginning of a New World Order, the U.S. military had premiered, live before a world television audience, a new kind of war: the high-tech, low-casualty rout of a tyrannical regime.

From the vantage point of a decade, the victory no longer appears so decisive or easily won. Tens of thousands of U.S. veterans say they have grown sick, and thousands may have died, from the stew of poisons to which they were exposed in the desert. The government has concluded that the military's highly touted smart weapons worked far less successfully than advertised, and some experts question whether the Patriots worked at all.

Iraqi President Saddam Hussein is still in power, menacing his people and threatening his neighbors. The United States remains deployed in the region, championing postwar sanctions and enforcing "no-fly" zones in what has become the longest U.S. military campaign since the Vietnam War. The standoff continues.

"The allied forces can claim that they achieved the very limited objectives their political masters set out for them," says Roger J. Spiller, George C. Marshall Professor of Military History at the U.S. Army Command and General Staff College. "But I think one can argue that hostilities continue even today."

The crisis began Aug. 2, 1990, when Hussein ordered his troops into neighboring Kuwait. Within days, Bush was organizing an international coalition to oppose Iraq, and massing a force that would include more than 4,000 soldiers from Connecticut -- National Guard members and reservists who left jobs and families to join regulars in Saudi Arabia.

Taking a lesson from history, Bush brought his case for war to the American public. Americans, divided over U.S. military involvement in Vietnam a generation earlier, tied yellow ribbons around trees, displayed bumper stickers urging "Support Our Troops" and wrote letters to soldiers in the desert.

The coalition struck on Jan. 17, 1991. For the next 5 1/2 weeks, the coalition pounded Iraq with more tons of explosives than the Allies dropped on Germany and Japan during World War II. By the time the allies stopped the bombing, it took ground troops just 100 hours to liberate Kuwait.

The U.S. military, which had braced for as many as 30,000 casualties, suffered 299 dead and 467 wounded. Eight of those killed - - seven men and one woman -- lived in or had long ties to Connecticut.

But the actual cost may have been much higher.

The official count does not include U.S. veterans who became sick after wading through the toxic soup of chemicals and radiation that was stirred when the coalition stormed through the desert. Before the war, Hussein ordered chemical weapons buried in the path of oncoming coalition troops. During the war, U.S. forces fired ammunition made with depleted uranium, a heavy-metal nuclear waste product that creates radioactive dust. At the end of the war, Iraqi troops set fire to Kuwaiti oilfields, creating poisonous fires that burned for weeks.

About 186,600 of the 528,663 gulf war veterans no longer in the service, or 32 percent, have applied for disability due to sicknesses or injuries, according to the U.S. Department of Veterans Affairs. More than 18,000 have neurological disorders. The average age of U.S. troops in the war was 28.

The Pentagon blames increases in sickness among gulf war veterans on the physical and emotional stress of combat. Over time, defense officials have acknowledged as many as 99,000 troops may have been exposed to low levels of nerve gas, but they say the levels were too low to cause harm.

James Tuite, a former congressional investigator, says thousands of gulf war veterans and perhaps millions of Iraqi civilians were exposed to unhealthy doses of chemical agents after coalition forces bombed Iraqi weapons plants. Pentagon-funded studies by Dr.

Robert Haley of the University of Texas suggest specific abnormalities in the brains of some gulf war veterans.

In addition, some scientists believe vaccines that were administered to protect troops from chemical and biological agents have themselves made many sick.

'A study of 2,030 gulf war-era veterans by the Kansas Commission on Veterans Affairs shows that 34 percent who served in the gulf have chronic illnesses, as do 12 percent who were inoculated but did not serve in the gulf. Just 4 percent of those who did not serve in the gulf and were not inoculated have chronic illnesses.''

''Observed patterns suggest that excess morbidity among Gulf War veterans is associated with characteristics of their wartime service, and that vaccines used during the war may be a contributing factor,'' says The American Journal of Epidemiology, Volume 152, Issue 10, 15 November 2000.

Troops from other coalition nations have reported varying rates of illnesses. A January 1999 study in the British medical journal The Lancet found British gulf war veterans had rates of ill health at least twice that of British veterans who stayed home, or were sent to Bosnia.

The reputation of the coalition's high-tech weaponry has fallen even as health complaints by gulf war veterans have climbed. In a 1997 study, the U.S. General Accounting Office found military officials and defense contractors overstated the effectiveness of Raytheon-produced Patriot missiles and smart bombs during the war.

"Data show clear success against the oil and electrical target categories, but less success against Iraqi air defense, command, control, and communications, and lines of communication," the nonpartisan congressional agency found. "Success against nuclear-related, mobile Scud, and Republican Guard targets was the least measurable."

During the war, Bush boasted Patriot missiles had shot down 41 of 42 Scuds fired at Israel and Saudi Arabia. Defense department officials later said the weapon actually knocked down perhaps 70 percent of the Scuds aimed at Saudi Arabia and 40 percent aimed at Israel. Other experts say the missile may not have scored more than one clean hit.

"It was in the interests of the United States and Israel that the Patriots be perceived as being better than they were," says retired U.S. Army Gen. James Terry Scott, now director of the national security program at Harvard's John F. Kennedy School of Government. "You have to understand the psychology of warfare. You want to make the enemy believe his weapons aren't working."

Kwai Chan, director of the GAO study, says increasing public expectation of surgical combat with precision munitions could fundamentally change our concept of war. There is the danger, he says, that if war comes to seem too clean or easy, it could become viewed as a tool of diplomacy, rather than the result of failed diplomacy.

U.S. commanders were able to promote the success of smart weapons in part because they controlled the release of information about the war. In the hostile desert environment, most reporters relied on the military for survival; for information, they were limited to the details that could be gleaned from media briefings or pool reports by colleagues under military escort.

"The Pentagon learned during the Vietnam War of the risks involved in letting people know what's going on," says former U.S. Rep. Lee Hamilton, who was chairman of the House International Affairs Committee. "The Bush administration managed the news very rigidly. In briefings on the hill, you could get information only from a few people -- Colin Powell, Dick Cheney, the president. No one else was allowed to talk."

The image of a smart war helped to obscure the grimmer picture that has emerged over time. On Feb. 13, 1991, coalition pilots fired two missiles at a civilian bomb shelter in a middle-class neighborhood of Baghdad, incinerating hundreds of Iraqis, mostly women and children. In 1992, Pentagon officials acknowledged that U.S. troops used earth moving equipment to bury thousands of Iraqi soldiers alive. Investigative reporter Seymour Hersh last summer revived allegations that a U.S. infantry division launched an unprovoked attack on defeated Iraqi soldiers as they retreated toward Baghdad in early March 1991, after the cease-fire.

Ten years after the 42-day war began, Iraq lies in ruin, its people devastated by a decade of sanctions that have slowed the import of food, medicine and spare parts to repair the power plants and water treatment facilities targeted by coalition bombers. The United Nations blames the embargo for the deaths of more than 1 million Iraqis.

Hussein lives in luxury, protected by billions of dollars and his loyal and well-armed Republican Guard. The United Nations withdrew its weapons inspectors after the regime stopped all access more than two years ago; Iraqi officials say they will not be allowed to return.

George W. Bush spoke during the presidential campaign of making sanctions "tougher," and said if he learned Iraq had obtained weapons of mass destruction, he'd "take 'em out."

Ten years after the start of the war, Bush comes to office facing pressure to resolve the conflict once and for all.

After retiring from The Courant in 2005, I instinctively could not stop investigative reporting. I began free-lancing work even though it immediately resulted extremely low compensation, no matter what publication I wrote for. I guess one has to be a famous writer to be properly compensated.

But freelance writing eventually led to one of the most interesting and high echelon targets I ever discovered, irregularities by U.S. President George W. Bush.

I wasn't the freelancer to discover the potential story line. Amazingly and by chance, I got the tip-off call from Western Connecticut State University Professor John P. Briggs. Decades earlier, Briggs and I had worked as reporters at The Hartford Courant and had co-authored a couple of police stories together.

He told me that he and his father had been working on investigating Bush for their own stories and had found a potential tale that could use my experience to help exploration. It involved Bush's right-wing religious beliefs, amazingly helping induce the United States' to go to war with Iraq.

Bush wanted to combat a country he considered part of an 'axis of evil' that were allegedly aligned with terrorists and posing a threat to U.S. interests through possession of "weapons of mass destruction."

But John Briggs explained that we needed to truly explore the president's deeply held religious motivations influencing his inspiration for this conflict. So we spent weeks looking at every angle of motivations for war through interviews and Internet searches. Amazingly, Bush's inter-religious communications with the right-wing End Time Christians, encouraging this war, were sitting there, right inside the White House's Internet site.

Here is what we eventually wrote for Truthout: Bush, Mideast Wars and End-Time Prophecy

By JP Briggs II, Ph. D., and Thomas D. Williams

Truthout | Special Report Friday 29 June 2007

"Religious institutions that use government power in support of themselves and force their views on persons of other faiths, or of no faith, undermine all our civil rights. Moreover, state support of an established religion tends to make the clergy unresponsive to their own people and leads to corruption within religion itself. Erecting the 'wall of separation between church and state,' therefore, is absolutely essential in a free society."

- Former US President Thomas Jefferson

President George W. Bush has become dangerously steeped in ideas of Armageddon, the Apocalypse, an imminent war with Satanic forces in the Middle East, and an urgency to construct an American theocracy to fulfill God's end-of-days plan, according to close observers.

Historians and investigative journalists following the "end-time Christian" movement have grown alarmed at the impact it may be having on Bush's Middle East policies, including the current war in Iraq, the ongoing Israeli-Palestinian crisis, the strife in Lebanon and the administration's repeated attempts to find a cause for war against Iran.

Many people are aware that Bush is "the most aggressively religious president in American History," as eminent historian Arthur Schlesinger Jr. described him, (Schlesinger, "War and the Presidency," 143) but most remain without a clue to what this actually means.

One piece of evidence is Bush's funneling billions of dollars to "faith-based" organizations. Faith offices making grants are now so widespread inside government agencies that federal watchdog officials have serious difficulties accounting for how much money has actually been spent.

(Goldberg, "Kingdom Coming" 121). Marvin Olasky, a devotee of end-time theology, designed Bush's faith-based welfare concept.

See also Goldberg, "Kingdom Coming," 110.

Further evidence is the Bush administration's transformation of the military. Until complaints forced its removal, a religious recruitment video made by a group called the Christian Embassy appeared on the Department of Defense web site.

The video included interviews made inside the Pentagon with seven high-ranking military officers, congressmen, other federal officials and even the Christian Ethiopian ambassador to the US about their personal relationship with Christ.

Army Lt. General William "Jerry" Boykin made headlines in 2003 when he said he believed America was engaged in a holy war as a "Christian nation" battling Satan. Adversaries can be defeated, he said, "only if we come against them in the name of Jesus." Despite his highly publicized rhetoric, Boykin remains Bush's deputy undersecretary of defense for intelligence.

Beneath Bush's benign-sounding words, "faith" and "Christian," lies the deeper reality of the authoritarian, doomsday religious beliefs of the ministers and spiritual counselors that surround him, say experts.

Officially he has been at pains to show an openness traditionally expected of an American president. Typical is his assertion in a speech at a National Prayer Breakfast found on the White House website: "There's another part of our heritage we are showing in Iraq, and that is the great American tradition of religious tolerance. The Iraqi people are mostly Muslims, and we respect the faith they practice."

However, experts point out the particular brand of Christianity that permeates Bush's environment is anything but tolerant. For example, Bush's own personal minister, Franklin Graham, has called Islam "evil and very wicked." He has said, "Let's use the weapons we have, the weapons of mass destruction if need be, and destroy the enemy."

Respected journalist Bill Moyers says that for the religious figures around Bush "a war with Islam in the Middle East is not something to be feared but welcomed - an essential conflagration on the road to redemption."

Scholars calculate that the group, which religion author Lynne Bundesen has dubbed "end-time Christians," has up to 40 million followers. Though not all may fully subscribe to the doomsday theology, they are inundated with it in books, megachurches, and on Christian broadcasting stations that reach millions upon millions of the faithful and are almost entirely dominated by end-time preachers.

The messages come from "dispensationalists," who believe that true believers are close to the time of being "raptured," or drawn up into heaven by God, in the days before the final battles. They also emanate from various stripes of "dominionists" pushing to erect an American theocracy for the end-of-the-world wars against the anti-Christ. Read "Who Are The End-Time Christians?"

Cross hairs Iran - an Illustration

A potent example of the influence of end-time Christians in the White House developed in early May 2007 when the president invited dominionist James Dobson and 12 or 13 other "family value" ministers for a special meeting. They were called in to discuss the "disturbing threats Iraq, Iran and international terrorism posed to US, Israel and other democracies around the world.

Dobson is best known as the founder of Focus on the Family, an end-time lobby. Dobson opposes homosexual rights and abortion and advocates the "submission of women." He has backed candidates who call for the execution of abortion providers and works to establish an American theocracy. Dobson was careful not to quote the president in his radio address.

He declined a Truthout interview request about his influential relationship with Bush, including what his radio broadcast said involved many meetings in the past with the president.

Dobson told his listeners that Bush "appeared upbeat and determined and convinced that his mission is to protect this great nation from those who have threatened us." He said Bush wanted "to let history be his judge for the way he has dealt with this crisis in the Middle East.... He laid out the challenge before us."

The meeting with Bush, said Dobson, inspired an entire week of his radio discussions on radical Islam's impact on America. He said the "general tenor and tone" of his session with the president emphasized "how we are living in very perilous times, and the future generations of Americans depends upon how we rise to that challenge today."

He continued: "Iran has promised to blow Israel off the face of the earth, and they have made no bones about that.... They fully intend to wage war with us. They will do it when they have the nuclear and biological weapons to do it."

On the same program, Dobson pointedly discussed the president and the Iranian "threat" with bestselling author and dispensationalist Joel Rosenberg.

Rosenberg is an end-time "prophecy expert" who claims he makes frequent visits to the White House to help them "understand what will happen next in the Middle East."

He informed Dobson's listeners that Iranian President Mahmoud Ahmadinejad - the latest in a long line of end-time anti-Christ candidates that recently included Saddam Hussein - is "telling people inside Iran that he believes that the end of the world is just two or three years away."

Dobson, referring to Ahmadinejad, said: "We didn't take Hitler very seriously either. I just see the parallel. The president, it seems to me, does understand this."

Divine Mission

From the beginning of his presidency, Bush's own messianic statements have been downplayed or dismissed by the mainstream press - uncertain of how seriously to take them and shy of offending the religious feeling of their Christian audience.

In "American Theocracy," historian Kevin Phillips, a former Republican strategist, explores the question of Bush's professed sense of "divine mission." "I trust God speaks through me. Without that, I couldn't do my job," the president told a gathering in 2004.

Phillips concludes that "the president of the United States may for some years have wandered into what we could describe as a period of personal theocracy, and he may have shaped US policy in the Middle East around a personal and radical interpretation of the Bible." (Phillips, "American Theocracy," XLII)

Former House Majority Leader Dick Armey told the BBC World Service in 2002 that he believed the president subscribed to end-time prophecies when "the whole world goes through a difficult time during those days of Tribulation."

Stephen Zunes, Middle East editor of the Foreign Policy in Focus project, observes that "Iraq has become the new Babylon" for Bush.

In biblical Revelation, Babylon is the "great whore" representing human sin and corruption that will be destroyed to allow Jerusalem's rise and Jesus's return.

In an unscripted moment talking to the troops in April 2007 - as Iraq descended into chaos and the Democrats pressed him to pull the troops out - Bush seemed to offer a view of biblical Babylon and prophetic Tribulations.

He said of Iraq: "It makes me realize the nature of the enemy that we face, which hardens my resolve to protect the American people. The people who do that are not people - you know, it's not a civil war; it is pure evil. And I believe we have an obligation to protect ourselves from that evil."

Paul S. Boyer, professor emeritus of history at the University of Wisconsin-Madison and author of "When Time Shall Be No More: Prophecy Belief in Modern American Culture," said in a lengthy telephone interview: "That sounds very much like Bush, kind of inarticulate, but also the workings of his mind are pretty clear. In his first speech after 9/11, he said he would rid the world of evil, which was an extreme evangelical sense of defining the war on terror."

Norton Mezvinsky, a distinguished CSU professor of history at Central Connecticut State University, has also extensively researched the Christian end-time movement and is writing a book on the subject.

In an interview in his office, he agreed the president's statement fits with his 9/11 pronouncements. "You knew Bush was saying he just got the message from God; he finally realized why he was president of the United States." Mezvinsky says, "There's no question that he is and has been influenced by the end-time ideas.... So there is a danger. To what extent? We don't know. The extent that we know is pretty bad."

A spokeswoman for the White House did not respond to nine requests by email and telephone for the president's answers to a series of questions about that influence.

But when Phillips's "American Theocracy" came out in March 2006, a questioner at a Bush speech referred to the historian's book and asked whether the president believed in the Apocalypse.

The Washington Post reported that Bush stammered and laughed nervously as he responded: "The answer is - I haven't really thought of it that way.... The first I've heard of that, by the way. I guess I'm more of a practical fellow."

Phillips writes in the new introduction to his book that Bush then went on with his answer for "four and a half minutes without ever mentioning the Apocalypse, Armageddon, the end-times, or the Book of Revelation." (Phillips, "American Theocracy," XL).

The Israel Connection

One of the most influential end-time Christian ministers with entree to the president is John Hagee.

Recently, Hagee updated his book, "Jerusalem Countdown," to highlight a coming war with Iran. It promises: "There will soon be a nuclear blast in the Middle East that will transform the road to Armageddon into a racetrack. America and Israel will either take down Iran or Iran will become nuclear and attempt to take down America and Israel."

Hagee claims Iran is producing nuclear "suitcase bombs."

In 2006, Hagee assembled a large number of end-time Christian groups into an umbrella organization, Christians United for Israel. When CUFI met for the first time in Washington, Israel had just invaded Lebanon. The British Telegraph newspaper reported that Hagee's "claim of political clout is no idle boast. The president sent a message of support praising him for 'spreading the hope of God's Love and the universal gift of freedom.'"

During the invasion period, www.raptureready.com, the website for those anticipating ascension into heaven before the final battles, excitement mushroomed. Responders thought the war in Lebanon signaled the start of the Tribulations. "This is so exciting," one commenterr (an isolated commentator) offered. "I have been having rapture dreams and I can't believe that this is really it! We are on the edge of eternity!"

Meanwhile, other websites noted the curious echo of prophecy from a statement by Secretary of State Condoleezza Rice that clearly grated on foreign diplomats' nerves: "What we're seeing here are the birth pangs of a new Middle East," she said, even as she refused to call for a cease fire to end the killing and destruction going on in Lebanon.

The echo was a core prophetic verse in Matthew: "And you will hear of wars and rumors of wars; see that you are not alarmed; for this must take place, but the end is not yet. For nation will rise against nation, and kingdom against kingdom, and there will be famines and earthquakes in various places: all this is but the beginning of the birth pangs." Was it a coincidence of language from a woman who has described herself as born again and evangelical? Rice denied any such reference.

Though they give different, sometimes changing "literal" versions of how close the Apocalypse is, end-timers all agree that the establishment of Israeli hegemony over the biblical lands and the rebuilding of the ancient Jewish temple are preconditions for Christ's return.

From this belief derives the unwavering support of end-time Christians for Israel. Both dominionists, who believe in a literal interpretation of the Bible, and dispensationalists, who hold to that literal interpretation, call themselves "Christian Zionists." End-time Christians (or Christian Zionists) have become Israel's main tourist revenue, shepherding groups to the holy land to see the sites of Armageddon and the Second Coming.

Mezvinsky has extensive contacts within the Israeli government and various conservative Israeli groups, and he is emphatic on one point: although a succession of Israeli prime ministers has courted the American end-timers (the Christian Zionists) and declared them Israel's "greatest friends," the Israelis don't accept the end-time theology one wit. They are also aware that it is anti-Semitic. (For one thing, they interpret the Bible as claiming that only 144,000 converted Jews will be allowed to survive the Apocalypse.)

However, Mezvinsky says, the Israelis also know that the end-time Christian Zionists are a lobby that can deliver US support for Israeli hard-line positions on arms, West Bank settlements, negotiations with the Arabs, and Iran.

Neocons and End-Timers

Historians Mezvinsky and Boyer stress that the power of blood-drenched, Satan-versus-God Christian prophecy has merged with another major factor shaping the Bush administration's Mideast policy and the current focus of hostility toward Iran.

As president, George W. Bush represents a perfect storm that has blown neoconservative ideology together with the end-time movement. Before 9/11, the neocons envisioned an American global empire supported by newly created democracies friendly to American interests in oil, markets and ideas. But they thought only a Pearl Harbor-type event like 9/11 would make mobilizing the country for it possible.

The key to this plan was the Middle East. Phillips says that designs on Middle East oil reserves, particularly in Iraq and Iran, were part of the neocon strategy. Notes Boyer, the neocons and end-timers "come at the subject of the Mideast war from different perspectives, but they end up agreeing."

In Bush's speeches, a careful coding of words and phrases also brings the neocon and end-time perspectives together. The president makes "liberty" and "democracy," for example, synonymous with "divine wishes." Read sidebar, "Hidden Behind Coded Language."

But Mezvinksy cautions that many neocon strategists probably think the end-time Christian Zionists "are nuts, but, boy, we can utilize them." Indeed, the thinly concealed disdain some neocons have expressed for the prophetic Christians has fed into the media habit of underestimating end-time influence on the assumption that only identifiable political ideas can shape police. Meanwhile, the influence of end-time Christians has burrowed deeply into the American Israel Political Action Committee, AIPAC, the powerful Israeli lobby. At the last AIPAC meeting with a long list of speakers that included Hillary Clinton and Barack Obama, "Hagee got the loudest applause of anybody," according to Mezvinsky.

Mezvinsky reports he is increasingly hearing Israelis say that "we want the United States focusing on Iran. Those are people who would like the United States to attack Iran. They realize that, given the involvement in Iraq, there's not the wherewithal to go after Iran." Israel Prime Minister Ehud Olmert has called Iran an "existential threat" to Israel.

This spring, AIPAC, with the help of its end-time supporters, succeeded in removing language from a military appropriations bill that would have required Bush to get Congressional approval before using military force against Iran.

So again, Iran policy provides the example - here for how end-time religion, the politics of Israel and neocon strategies converge. And how end-time thinking entangles George W. Bush.

At about the same period that Bush was meeting with Dobson and Dobson was touting a war with Iran, Vice President Dick Cheney, the consummate neocon (no sign on his horizon of end-time religious views), stood on the deck of an American aircraft carrier just off Iran's coast.

He warned that the United States was prepared to use its naval power to keep Tehran from disrupting oil routes or "gaining nuclear weapons."

But, a Cheney spokesperson cited his remarks on the aircraft carrier, as mentioned word-for-word on the White House Internet site, to suggest there is no warning to use naval power against Iran.

The Kuwait Times reported that Cheney had visited the region to forge an alliance among the United Arab Emirates, Jordan and Egypt "in support of a possible US strike against Iran over its controversial nuclear program, according to Jordanian politicians and academics." Cheney was apparently unsuccessful, the newspaper said.

When asked about his foreign policy position on Iran, a Cheney spokesperson cited a statement from Cheney: "We hope that we can solve the problem diplomatically. The president has indicated he wants to do everything he can to resolve it diplomatically. That is why we've been working with the EU (European Union) and going through the United Nations with sanctions. But the president has also made it clear that we haven't taken any options off the table."

The Cheney aide's references to Cheney statements made no mention about "a strike on Iran."

For probably different reasons, the fascination of Bush and Cheney for war with Iran has been longstanding. Reports say Secretary of Defense Donald Rumsfeld's original war plans for Iraq included moving on to Iran within 90 days of securing Baghdad.

The plans were later dropped, but they suited both neocon adventure for oil and democratization and the violent Christian prophecy that sees defeat of Babylon as a vital step on the path to the return of Christ. (Dubose and Bernstein, Vice 182) Through it all, nuclear bombs convey the awe of an Apocalypse.

In the spring of 2006, Pulitzer prize journalist Seymour Hersh reported Bush had ordered his generals to begin planning for an air assault on Iran's nuclear facilities using "bunker-busting" tactical nuclear weapons.

When generals tried to remove the nuclear option from the plans, they were "shouted down," Hersh wrote. Said a former senior intelligence official, "Bush and Cheney were dead serious about the nuclear planning." There were also reports the administration was trying to convince the Israelis to do the bombing.

Then in late February this year, new word came on Bush's Iran war planning. The London Times reported:

"Some of America's most senior military commanders are prepared to resign if the White House orders a military strike against Iran, according to highly placed defense and intelligence sources. Tension in the Gulf region has raised fears that an attack on Iran is becoming increasingly likely before President George Bush leaves office. The Sunday Times has learned that up to five (US) generals and admirals are willing to resign rather than approve what they consider would be a reckless attack. 'There are four or five generals and admirals we know of who would resign if Bush ordered an attack on Iran,' a source with close ties to British intelligence said. 'There is simply no stomach for it in the Pentagon, and a lot of people question whether such an attack would be effective or even possible. "

In May 2007, the Inter Press Service reported that Admiral William J. Fallon, who was slated to become the Central Command chief on March 16, had sent a message to the Defense Department in mid-February, opposing any further US naval buildup in the Persian Gulf. The news article said Fallon squelched an administration effort to send a third carrier strike group to the Gulf.

That would have brought the US naval presence up to the same level as during the US air campaign against the Saddam Hussein regime in Iraq, the report said. It continued: "A source who met privately with Fallon around the time of his confirmation hearing and who insists on anonymity quoted Fallon as saying that an attack on Iran 'will not happen on my watch.'

Asked how he could be sure, the source says, Fallon replied, 'You know what choices I have. I'm a professional.' Fallon said that he was not alone, according to the source, adding, "There are several of us trying to put the crazies back in the box."

Of course, no one knows if the administration will eventually attack Iran. But experts believe that end-time ideas are playing a part in Bush's thinking about a widening war in the region.

End Game

Bundesen's sources within the religious community and in the military around the president tell her that end-timers are "crawling all over the White House and Camp David." These are men who purvey what Hedges calls a "theology of despair" that "feeds dark fantasies of revenge and empowerment.

Bundesen says she is not being cynical when she observes that end-time ministers like the late Jerry Falwell, Pat Robertson, John Hagee, Tim LaHaye and James Dobson have used their dark theology to increase their followers, pump up their power and fill their coffers.

And it's clear that Bush, in turn, has used end-time Christian leaders and their ideas for political and moral support. So isn't it just about politics?

No. Experts say that whether anybody even believes the violently apocalyptical scenarios predicting disaster should not obscure the stark fact that Bush's policies have emerged in an atmosphere saturated with these dark ideas. Journalist Ron Suskind reported in 2004 that the administration prided itself on not being "reality-based," and the end-time vision may be one way to understand what that pride is about.

CHAPTER 15

ANTHRAX VACCINE CREATES INCREDIBLE HEALTH PROBLEMS DURING AND AFTER THE GULF WAR

One of the toughest series of investigative tales I faced in my long career at The Courant was exposing the causes of mysterious sicknesses resulting from hazardous Gulf War exposures, as well as faulty preparations for those exposures.

Ironically, one of the most dangerous of these potential weapons, menacing during the first and second initiations of the Gulf War, were Anthrax spores, feared fired from warheads and in aerial or aerosolized attacks.

I say "tale" because the effort on behalf of the Department of Defense was a fiction of sorts. It was a façade or pretense to imply our troops were protected by the anthrax vaccine against a potentially deadly weaponized bacteria. It was even more so a patently deceptive fiction to assert the U.S. produced vaccine, intended to protect the troops, was safe, effective and FDA approved. It was none of those things.

What was not a fiction involved the very real illnesses the improperly approved and illegal investigational vaccine caused amongst our troops. Dangerously and illegally, they were actually captive guinea pigs for this historically unprecedented experiment.

Here is what an Active Post article By Catherine J. Frompovich said about the vaccine: "Thirty percent of those vaccinated in the military confirmed vaccine damage, aka Gulf War Syndrome. Many military careers—especially pilots—ended due to Anthrax vaccine damage. It was common knowledge in the services that vaccines were getting harmed and sick after taking the Anthrax vaccine." https://www.activistpost.com/2016/06/the-u-s-military-personnels-smoking-gun-documentation-regarding-the-anthrax-vaccine.html

The National Vaccine Information Center says anthrax spores are germs that can adversely impact upon crops and sicken or kill people, or livestock, by typically affecting the skin and lungs. They are a biological agent said to have been ready for deadly spreading by the Iraqis. It can be weaponry transmitted to humans, says the center, causing severe skin ulceration (malignant pustule) or a form of pneumonia (wool-sorters' disease).

Then, outrageously, the most serious anthrax vaccine reactions are frightening. They result in permanent autoimmune and brain dysfunction. As have been reported, ever dangerous backlashes include chronic disabling fatigue, persistent headaches, severe joint pain and crippling arthritis, numbness, muscle weakness, and severe memory loss, paralysis, brain inflammation, seizures and death. See https://www.nvic.org/Vaccines-and-Diseases/Anthrax.aspx

"If left untreated with antibiotics, lethal toxins from the anthrax bacteria can multiply in the body and kill quickly," says The National Vaccine Center. However, the U.S. military intelligence says, they were used turned out to be fictitious. Anthrax's contrived use by the Iraqis created fear for the safety of U.S. troops that was not unraveled for both wars in the Gulf.

The UCLA School of Public Health says: ''Iraq purchased anthrax spores from the United States in the 1980s, and was thought to be developing the capability to use them in warheads and in aerial attacks…After the (second Iraqi) war, the UN Special Commission on Iraq (UNSCOM) destroyed the remaining production and stockpiling facilities for biological warfare in Iraq. 'By 1998, we were able to establish that Iraq had no capability of producing biological weapons,' a former UN inspector, Scott Ritter, told the BBC.' ''

See http://www.ph.ucla.edu/epi/bioter/anthraxasweapon.html

However, shockingly, that late discovery became chancy and fearsome for thousands of US troops who were vaccinated for protection. That anthrax vaccine was first manufactured by Michigan Biologic Products Institute, the last state-owned vaccine laboratory in the United States.

The New York Times reported in July1998 that the vaccine was sold to that newly formed company, the BioPort Corporation. "It had an inside track on at least $60 million in Pentagon contracts for anthrax vaccine to protect the nation's 2.4 million members of the armed forces and reservists against an anthrax attack," The Times reported.

Just two years later, here is official overwhelmingly negative evaluation of that very program: "In 2000 The Office of the Inspector General of the Department of Defense, issues an audit report D-2000-105, reporting that over $2 million in taxpayer funds advanced to BioPort were not spent on improvements to vaccine production…The Full Committee on Government Reform adopts the Subcommittee report recommending suspension of the Anthrax Vaccine Immunization Program."

The Department of Defense utilized that vaccine supposedly to protect troops before they were exposed to spores. But, instead, the drug ultimately became seriously debilitating and even deadly for many.

The vaccine was first used widespread during the first Gulf War in 1991. The mandatory vaccinations began again for the entire armed forces in 1997. It was not until 2003 that the vaccine's use was halted by an injunction from Federal Judge Emmett Sullivan. He ruled the vaccine had never been properly FDA licensed. Incapable of admitting its extensive past errors, the Defense Department renewed use of the vaccine in 2007, after the immunization finally received a formal FDA approval.

The two most dedicated military pilots to stand up against the Pentagon for its mandatory anthrax vaccine policies were U.S. Navy Major Russell E. Dingle and Lt. Col. Thomas L. Rempfer. Russ is shown above and Tom below.

They risked all potential promotions or revengeful military discipline while fighting against compulsory use of that extremely dangerous anthrax vaccine. Despite their opposition to the vaccine program, these two men were promoted multiple times, while other vaccine-opposing troops of lower rank received inequitable disciplines to include fines, dishonorable discharges, demotions and jail time.

Rempfer and Dingle, recognized the incredible health danger to service members, making thousands of them seriously ill. As a result, they began incredible protest battles with the Pentagon while collecting evidence, interviewing victims and pressing constant complaints to the Pentagon and other relevant federal agencies.

Since they were ordered to resign from the Guard in January 1999 in protest over the Guard's refusal to accept their findings about the vaccine, Dingle and Rempfer had been among a dozen leaders in a national protest effort to stop the use of the vaccine.

Tragically, for all he helped over the years, Dingle died of cancer on September 4, 2005. Lt. Col. Russ Dingle's career as an Air Force Officer and Fighter Pilot included over 2,000 hours on active duty in the A-10 Thunderbolt II, a single-seat, twin turbofan engine, straight wing jet aircraft. He served as an Instructor Pilot and a Flight Commander for the Connecticut Air National Guard, earning multiple awards as "Top Gun."

Russ was selected to both lead a flight of those A-10's in the U.S. Air Force Gun smoke competition in 1993, and support the United Nation's peacekeeping mission over Bosnia in 1996. Lt. Col. Dingle's career was also uniquely distinguished by his noble advocacy for soldier's health rights, testifying as an expert witness for the U.S. Congress in 1999, as well as serving as an expert for the Government Accountability Office and the Connecticut Attorney General's Office.

Russ' exemplary career included over 16 years of service as a pilot and Captain for American Airlines in the Boeing 767, 737, and S-80. He will always be remembered as the intellectual force behind accountability efforts on the anthrax vaccine.

A dedication in his honor goes on to say, "His family, as well as his fellow citizens and soldiers, miss him dearly, but will eternally benefit from his life's accomplishments, courage, service, leadership, and most importantly, his honor."

The effort for correction of military records for troops wrongfully punished in the effort to bully compliance with the vaccine mandate is chronicled at this website: https://hoping4justice.com/about

From the 1997 to 2008-time frame I published over 70 articles dedicated to this investigative topic. The initial objections about the vaccine brought forth by Dingle and Rempfer were ultimately validated by GAO findings, Congressional reports and Federal court rulings. Here is Rempfer's Internet site explaining the ongoing effort to obtain record corrections for troops punished over the anthrax vaccine: https://hoping4justice.com/

When the officers objected to the vaccine mandate, as required by the Uniform Code of Military Justice (UCMJ), for patently illegal orders, they were besmirched by their chain of command all the way up to the Pentagon. Their dutiful objections were instead falsely framed as an attempt to avoid deployment.

As well, DOD officials made deceptive diversions, instead of corrections, about Internet disinformation regarding the vaccine. In fact, the only major actual disinformation on the subject was misinformation by the DoD officials.

What the DoD failed to be honest about was: the fact that the manufacturer had failed Food and Drug Administration (FDA) inspections prior to the launch of the 1998 mandatory program; and was issued a Notice of Intent to Revoke (NOIR) the vaccine license by the FDA. The DOD was not truthfully warning that the vaccine was considered experimental.

As well, the DOD did not confess that it and the manufacturer colluded by failing to obtain approval for major manufacturing changes to the vaccine prior to the first Gulf War. Additionally, the DOD failed to admit the Investigational New Drug (IND) application, filed with the FDA prior to the mandatory program, rendered that mandate illegal.

The anthrax vaccine manufacturer's September 20, 1996 Investigational New Drug application required the DOD to obtain informed consent from the troops, not forcing them into the mandatory program.

These revelations were brought to the attention of the FDA based on the evidence Dingle and Rempfer had provided through a Title 21 (21CFR10.30) Citizen Petition, which was filed at the Food and Drug Administration's headquarters in Rockville, Maryland on October 15, 2001.

Subsequently, a federal judge's preliminary injunction, citing the Citizen Opinion, halted the mandatory anthrax vaccine program. That opinion occurred over two years after the Citizen Petition's filing on December 22, 2003.

Just over a year and a month later, the same court ruled that "the involuntary anthrax vaccination program, as applied to all persons, is "rendered illegal absent informed consent." The court added that the anthrax vaccine license was to be vacated and the case remanded back to the FDA until a properly licensed immunization was accomplished.

That full approval did not occur until December 19, 2005. At that time the fully legal and approved status of the vaccine for the investigational use was approved by the FDA. Prior to that date the anthrax vaccine program was illegal.

Ironically, after these many prior years of controversy, on that very same October 15, 2001 date, the negligently designed vaccine, as well as the military-forced inoculation policy received, were only saved from cancellation based on the anthrax letter attacks of 2001.

On that very date, the anthrax laced letters were opened, being the second salvo of anthrax laced letters, within the office of Senator Tom Daschle.

Unbelievably, at the very same time they opened the anthrax letter, Rempfer was on the phone with Senator Daschle's staff informing them he'd personally delivered the Citizen Petition to FDA headquarters. But, the office informed Rempfer they were evacuating the office, and hung up on him.

Then, within days, Rempfer reported his suspicions to the FBI. He complained that someone inside the DOD might be responsible for the anthrax letter attacks since Senator Daschle was a major player in challenging the anthrax vaccine program and calling for records reviews for the troops.

Senator Daschle had personally coauthored a letter with Rep. Dick Gephardt four months earlier directly to the Secretary of Defense, Donald Rumsfeld, chronicling their objections to the vaccine program.

Sen Daschle was not the only high-level political figure challenging the vaccine program. Representative Christopher Shays led the early oversight of the vaccine, publishing a Congressional report titled "Unproven Force Protection."

Here is what Shays had to say to The Courant:

SHAYS REBUKES MILITARY ON ANTHRAX VACCINE

THOMAS D. WILLIAMS; Courant Staff Writer

U.S. Rep. Chris Shays, R-4th District, is challenging the emergency authorization that has allowed the Pentagon to vaccinate service members with a controversial anthrax vaccine because he said he believes that there is no immediate threat of the use of anthrax against the military.

Shays said he is dissatisfied with the U.S. Department of Health and Human Services' written responses to a series of questions he asked about the safety and effectiveness of the vaccine.

Anthrax spores sent through the mail in 2001 killed five people and sickened 17, but investigators found no evidence that it was an attack on the military. They also found that the anthrax spores were derived from a strain produced in the 1980s at the United States Army Medical Research Institute of Infectious Diseases in Maryland.

The adverse reaction rate of the vaccine is 100 times the figure initially stated by the vaccine's manufacturer. Adverse reactions include immune disorders, muscle and joint pain, headaches, rashes, fatigue, nausea, diarrhea, chills and fever. At least half a dozen deaths and a number of birth defects have been attributed to its use. More than 100 service members have been court-martialed for refusing the vaccine, 500 have been punished, and at least 300 pilots left the service after being told that they must be vaccinated.

"The HHS response states factual and legal conclusions not supported by anything yet on the public record," Shays said. "The process authorizing emergency use of a vaccine otherwise banned by a federal court should have been far more transparent."

The House Subcommittee on National Security, Emerging Threats and International Relations, of which Shays is chairman, expects to hold hearings this spring to determine whether HHS had the authority to permit emergency use of the vaccine.

In a letter to Shays, HHS Assistant Secretary Stewart Simonson said that the U.S. Food and Drug Administration approved the emergency use of a safe and effective vaccine and that the Department of Defense insisted that there was, in fact, an emergency need for inoculations. Simonson said HHS was satisfied that it had done all it could to publish notice of the emergency use and comply with all rules applying to it.

A hearing is scheduled for Friday in Washington before U.S. District Court Judge Emmet Sullivan, and Shays said he anticipates that it will yield more information for the committee to work with. Sullivan, who ordered the Pentagon to stop mandating anthrax inoculations for service members on Oct. 27, is expected to rule whether the Defense Department is in contempt of court for failing to abide by his order. The military vaccinated another 931 soldiers before stopping, a U.S. Justice Department document says.

Sullivan has said that the "investigational" vaccine's use without the "informed consent" of those receiving it or a presidential waiver is illegal. Although the FDA had not given the public an opportunity to make "meaningful comments" on the vaccine as required by law, it has since done so and is expected to re-verify that drug is safe and effective against airborne anthrax spores.

Robert Kramer Sr., president and chief operating officer of BioPort Corp., the vaccine's manufacturer in Lansing, Mich., said that the vaccine is not only proved safe and effective, but that it is the only means available to save the lives of service members faced with a biological attack from anthrax spores.

Separately from this article, as well, Connecticut's Attorney General, Richard Blumenthal, who would later become a Senator himself, also challenged Rumsfeld about the vaccine, based on his work with Dingle and Rempfer.

Blumenthal wrote to the DOD to "cease and desist your illegal conduct" several months prior to the anthrax attacks. It was in December 2000, when Blumenthal informed The Courant that he would present evidence produced by Dingle and Rempfer to the U.S. Food and Drug Administration to attempt convincing the agency the vaccine isn't properly licensed. He explained that he believes the irregular use of the vaccine could make Connecticut legally responsible for those who get sick from the vaccine.

As well, Karl Rove, who served as Special Assistant to President George W. Bush, had also connected with Rempfer and Dingle. After receiving their briefing in early 2001, he initiated a DOD internal investigation about the "political problems" associated with the vaccine and the historic Gulf War Illnesses.

Just prior to the anthrax attacks in August 2001, DOD Undersecretaries "Pete" Aldridge and Dr. David Chu recommended that Rumsfeld effectively cancel the vaccine's use. They suggested developing a modern immunization, exactly as Dingle and Rempfer recommended to their chain of command, during their original official tasking in 1997.

It was not until almost a decade after the anthrax attacks, in February 2010, that the FBI and DOJ would officially rule that the anthrax letter attacks were carried out by Bruce E. Ivins. He was an Army bio-defense expert who had committed suicide in 2008. As well, Ivins was a DOD scientist responsible for the anthrax vaccine testing at the US Army's laboratory on Fort Detrick.

Ivins motive, according to federal investigators, was to save the failing anthrax vaccine program. That potential motive was exactly what Rempfer had warned the FBI about almost ten years earlier.

Instead of admitting the relevance of these ignored tips in 2010, the FBI was less than forthright with the American people. The FBI's final report claimed that they found "no ostensible connection" for why Sen Daschle was attacked. The report claimed that witnesses had "no inkling" either.

However, the FBI knew this was not true. The FBI had been warned as to the motive for the attacks ten years earlier. To admit the tips about the exact source point of the attacks would have reflected poorly on the FBI's conduct in the case. Such conduct actually cost the American taxpayers $5.8 million in damages in work costs due to the Bureau's misdirects of suspicion toward an innocent person of earlier interest.

Following is a summary of the January 20, 2000, Rempfer opinion piece inside The Hartford Courant about the beginnings of what seemed like endless ignorance of a sickening, sometimes deadly, vaccine use. While the anthrax vaccine supposedly protected service members, its injections actually helped the enemy eliminate healthy soldiers.

In the year 2000, Rempfer wrote:

"''Two years ago, in 1998, Secretary of Defense William Cohen announced the Anthrax Vaccine Immunization Program for all service members. The policy was an effort to protect our nation's armed forces from the threat of inhaled anthrax produced by a biological weapon.''

''The vaccine was approved in 1970 for limited use to protect veterinarians and animal industry workers. The approval of this vaccine was based on a study of a different anthrax formulation found to be protective for topical or skin exposure to the disease.'

''The FDA has consistently found that no meaningful assessment has been made of the vaccine's effectiveness in humans against inhalation anthrax. Additionally, the General Accounting Office reported that the long-term safety of the vaccine has not yet been studied. To date, only about 15 percent of the military has received vaccinations, while hundreds have been discharged, punished or court-martialed for refusing.''

And here is the story about how two brave officers fought the battles against the Pentagon to protect servicemen from the continuous vaccine mandates.

Anthrax Avengers Connecticut Guardsmen risked careers to fight vaccine

By THOMAS D. WILLIAMS

U.S. Air Force Reserve Major Thomas "Buzz" Rempfer could be nearing the end of a decade-long battle with the Pentagon over the legality, safety and effectiveness of anthrax vaccines given to tens of thousands of military personnel.

He and others have won several favorable federal court rulings, one of which temporarily invalidated the original Defense Department order requiring vaccinations.

But Rempfer, 43, has paid a price. The former Connecticut National Guard pilot claims he was driven from his unit because of his opposition to the drug. And so his final legal battle is over whether he should be awarded damages to compensate him for lost pay and promotions.

The matter is before a panel called the Air Force Board for the Correction of Military Records, which is expected to rule on the case any time now.

Rempfer, a onetime West Suffield resident who now lives in Arizona, said he is less interested in his fortunes than those of others. He has repeatedly said that he and his now-deceased friend, U.S. Air Force Reserve Major Russell "Russ" E. Dingle, had been standing up for thousands of service members who were made ill by the vaccine or the hundreds punished for refusing to take it.

Rempfer is acting as a representative of Dingle's East Hartford estate. If the Air Force panel rules in their favor, the simple legal question will be: how can two military officers win monetary damages and nullify their punishments for refusing the vaccine without others being cleared as well?

In more than five years of research, Dingle and Rempfer concluded the anthrax vaccine was improperly licensed and ineffective. They found the vaccine, administered in six doses over 18 months, created thousands of adverse reactions. They concluded that the threat of a foreign anthrax attack is remote, and that if there ever is such an attack, those exposed can be protected by taking a regimen of antibiotics after the fact.

Along the way, Rempfer has made friends in high places. Among his backers: U.S. Rep. Christopher Shays, R-Fourth Dist., and Connecticut Attorney General Richard Blumenthal, who entered the fray three years ago by filing a friend of the court brief in a federal lawsuit brought by six service members challenging the vaccine.

At that time, Blumenthal said: "Major Rempfer has performed an extraordinary public service, a very noble and significant service in alerting the nation to the dangers of the anthrax vaccine at a time of tremendous stress on our military. He has unquestioned expertise and skill as well as impressive dedication and patriotism.'"

Anthrax History

Anthrax is a deadly bacteria that, in its natural form, is most often found in grass eating mammals, such as sheep and cattle. But it can also be manufactured in laboratories and used in biological weapons.

Anthrax became a household word in 2001 when, just after September 11 attacks, five people (including an Oxford, Conn., woman) were killed and 17 others sickened by anthrax sent through the mail. Among the recipients were the offices of two U.S. senators and a number of media organizations. The incidents are still under FBI investigation; authorities now believe the culprits are as-yet-unknown employees in a U.S. military laboratory.

But the anthrax vaccine dates back more than 40 years, when it was largely used by agricultural workers, veterinarians and wool industry workers. It had been manufactured to protect people against skin-to-skin contact with infected farm animals. Yet, the military has used it to protect service members against inhaled, manufactured anthrax spores spread by enemy explosions or devices.

Former Defense Secretary William Cohen and other federal officials supporting the new use of the vaccine have pointed to successful scientific tests with animals, even though some years earlier, when Cohen was in the Senate, he had participated in a congressional probe that concluded that the vaccine was unproven.

The drug's manufacturer – a company once known as BioPort Corp. and now called Emergent BioSolutions, of Rockville, Md. — insist the vaccine is safe and effective. That position is endorsed by the U.S. Food and Drug Administration and the Pentagon. But, that controversy dates to the 1991 Gulf War, when scores of service members complained of adverse reactions to the vaccine.

And so there was some resistance when Cohen ordered all 2.4 million service members to be inoculated in October 1998. Col. Walter Burns, then commander of the 103rd Fighter Wing of the Connecticut Air National Guard, created a two-man team – Rempfer and Dingle — to investigate the history, safety and legality of the anthrax vaccine.

After months of intensive research, the pilots concluded that the vaccine was improperly licensed and a potential health danger to troops. In light of the findings, a half dozen National Guard pilots rejected the vaccine and, they maintain, were forced out of the Guard in January 1999.

Rempfer and Dingle claim that Burns, bowing to political pressure, switched his position on the vaccine and also pressured them to resign. Blumenthal tried to force reinstatements of the pilots. But then-State Adjutant Gen. William Cugno denied the request, and Gov. M. Jodi Rell declined to overrule him.

Rempfer and Dingle switched to the Air Force Reserve, where they received promotions from superiors. Rempfer continues to fly today. Dingle died of cancer in September 2005 at age 49. His career included more than 16 years as a pilot and captain for American Airlines and 21 years as an instructor pilot and flight commander in the Air Force.

Rempfer, who is writing a book on the vaccine dispute, has always credited Dingle with performing the critical research on anthrax. "Lt. Col. Dingle's career," Rempfer wrote in an obituary, "was uniquely distinguished by his noble advocacy for soldier's health rights, testifying as an expert witness for the U.S. Congress in 1999, as well as serving as an expert for the Government Accounting Office and the Connecticut Attorney General's Office. We will eternally benefit from his life's accomplishments, courage, service, leadership, and most importantly, his honor."

Adverse Reactions

Rempfer and Dingle began their effort to clear their names in the U.S. Court of Claims. The case was soon refiled in federal court in 2003 and, later, sent to Air Force adjudicators.

The thrust of the case was that the vaccine had been improperly licensed because it had been manufactured to prevent infection from skin-to-skin contact but was being used to guard against inhalation of anthrax spores. The pilots also argued that the vaccine was unsafe, and listed adverse reactions including immune disorders, muscle and joint pains, headaches, rashes, fatigue, nausea, diarrhea, chills and fever.

The U.S. Government Accounting Office would later report that the vaccine's adverse reaction rate was 100 times higher than the 0.2 percent rate listed on the product's label.

But during federal court arguments in 2005, Ronald Wiltsie, a U.S. Justice Department lawyer, said that those challenging the vaccine "seek to undermine a key component of military readiness and defense against battlefield use of biological weapons." "There are risks with all vaccines, your honor," he said.

"The risks here are no greater than a tetanus shot or MMR, measles, mumps and rubella shots." Wiltsie also said the government did not rush to discipline those who refused to take the vaccine. He said anyone who initially declined was counseled by a medical professional. Only if they continued to refuse were they subject to sanctions, which included fines, court marshals, or being removed from the service.

Former Connecticut National Guard pilot Russell E. Dingle (left) and his friend Thomas Rempfer challenged the safety and effectiveness of an anthrax vaccine administered to military personnel. Their long legal battle against the Pentagon may be nearing its end.

Rempfer, Dingle and other service members were represented by attorneys John J. "Lou" Michels, who is a partner in the Chicago office of McGuireWoods, and Mark S. Zaid, managing partner in the Washington, D.C., firm of Krieger and Zaid.

"The basic legal argument [for the plaintiffs]," said Michels, who has handled the case pro bono, "was that the FDA failed to follow its own procedure in certifying that the anthrax vaccine was properly licensed for its intended purpose as a preventative against inhalation anthrax.

The court noted that the original medical expert panel assembled by the FDA to review the licensing standards for vaccines found that there was insufficient evidence to support a claim that the anthrax vaccine worked against inhalation anthrax."

In April 2005, U.S. District Court Judge Emmet Sullivan issued his decision. He temporarily halted the mandatory vaccinations. He declared that the vaccine was being used for an unapproved purpose and thus was "an investigational drug."

That meant, he said, only soldiers, sailors and airmen who gave consent could be vaccinated. The judge's edict required that service members be told about the drug's possible side effects.

Finally, he remanded the complaint back to the FDA to remedial action concerning the licensing of the vaccine. The FDA eventually made licensing adjustments to comply with Sullivan's orders, and after a hiatus, allowed mandatory vaccinations to restart.

The mandatory inoculations continue today, even though Rempfer and seven other service members brought another federal lawsuit challenging the FDA's licensing decision. Their challenge was rejected Feb. 29 by U.S. District Court Judge Rosemary M. Collyer, who ruled the FDA had not acted "arbitrarily or capriciously."

Air Force Panel

As the federal case moved forward, so did a separate effort by Dingle and Rempfer to win compensation before the Air Force Board for the Correction of Military Records. But in March 2006, the panel denied the claims.

Rempfer returned to federal court to appeal the decision.

On March 14, Washington, D.C., U.S. District Judge James Robertson ruled that the Air Force panel failed to properly consider the evidence before it. Specifically, he said, the board wrongly characterized the 2003 lawsuit as a victory for the government, when it was not. Robertson ordered the Air Force board to reconsider the request to nullify punishment and order back pay.

"Two federal judges have now confirmed the Pentagon broke the law by forcing service members to take anthrax vaccine from 1998 to late 2005," said retired Air Force Lt. Col. John Richardson, a North Carolina resident, former Gulf War pilot and an outspoken supporter of Rempfer and Dingle.

"Since 2005," Richardson said, "mandating the vaccine is now lawful only because of the FDA's willingness to ignore clear evidence in military medical records of the deaths and disabilities associated with the anthrax vaccine."

Rempfer does not want to comment about the imminent ruling by the Air Force panel, though another rejection could send him back to federal court. He said full attention now must be paid to restoring the honor and the health of all the servicemen and women who were punished for refusing to take the vaccine, or who became sick from it.

And so the last word goes to Dingle, Rempfer's departed friend, who considered both the vaccination program and the punishments to be unjust. He wrote: "When the U.S. military no longer allows for professional dissent within its ranks; when the U.S. military mandates that any and all orders be obeyed regardless of their moral or legal basis; when the U.S. military allows its members to defend themselves with 'I was just following orders', then the U.S. military will cease to attract men and women of principal and honor."

Here's the original news account with the details of why the anthrax vaccine was temporarily stopped after years of its negligent and ugly false usage, allegedly to save service members' health.

FDA HALTS USE OF OLD ANTHRAX VACCINE: [6/7 SPORTS FINAL Edition]

Williams, Thomas D; Courant Staff Writer. Hartford Courant; Hartford, Conn. [Hartford, Conn] 19 Oct 2002: B4.

As the U.S. gears up for a potential confrontation with Iraq, the U.S. Food and Drug Administration has halted use of older lots of the military's anthrax vaccine, and officials acknowledge that the vaccine is riskier than once thought.

In August, the FDA acknowledged that the vaccine manufacturer's license needed to be updated. That was seven months after the agency ordered that new warnings for consumers be included in the vaccine's insert package. It said the vaccine could harm people with immunity disorders, could cause a host of serious long-term adverse reactions and could already be responsible for six deaths and a number of birth defects.

The warnings, developed from complaints by military vaccine users since 1998, state that adverse reactions are expected in 5 percent to 35 percent of people who take the injection. That compares with the previous expected rate of 0.2 percent, established many years ago.

But the label represents more than a simple warning. It is tantamount to an FDA admission of a licensing problem that began in 1985 and remains unresolved today (October 2002).

The Department of Defense has said it is developing a new anthrax vaccine to respond to the concerns connected to the one in use now, but it asserts that the vaccine is both safe and effective.

In 1985, the FDA began reviewing the anthrax vaccine's manufacturing process to ensure it complied with federal rules for drugs. Recently, the FDA conceded to two Connecticut Air Force Reserve pilots that the review was never completed. The FDA told Maj. Russell Dingle and Maj. Thomas Rempfer that it would accomplish this, but didn't set a deadline to do so.

Dingle, of East Hartford, and Rempfer, of Suffield, who jointly filed a citizen petition with the FDA and a federal lawsuit against the manufacturer challenging the vaccine, said they don't truly expect the FDA to review the process again. That is because if the agency does, they said, it will have to stop licensing the drug.

The central problem is that the drug was never properly tested, said the two pilots, who have been researching the drug since they were ordered to take it while in the Air National Guard in 1998.

Manufacturers apply for drug licenses with the FDA after testing their products on volunteers. The FDA reviews the tests, the vaccine's safety and effectiveness and the manufacturing process before approving the license to manufacture the vaccine.

In 1970, Merck, a pharmaceutical company, obtained the initial federal license to produce the anthrax vaccine. It eventually stopped manufacturing the drug.

In the 1970s and 1980s, the Pentagon began sponsoring the manufacturing of the vaccine through the state of Michigan's health department. It used the old Merck testing data, collected from volunteers working in sheep wool mills, to justify the safety and effectiveness of the Michigan-manufactured vaccine.

Because the FDA never properly scrutinized this testing, and because the manufacturing process was changed in 1990, said Dingle and Rempfer, the drug simply is not properly licensed.

And its latest adverse reaction rate, they said, shows the vaccine is indeed different from the one tested by Merck.

In 1998, BioPort Corp. of Lansing, Mich., purchased the state of Michigan's manufacturing operation and all of its vaccine, then used it to inoculate the first 500,000 of the 2.4 million service members ordered to take it. In the meantime, BioPort sought approval to produce its own new batches of the vaccine.

In January, the FDA approved BioPort's facilities and its vaccine manufacturing processes after four years of failed federal inspections and infusion of millions of more taxpayer dollars for plant improvements.

As a result of Dingle's and Rempfer's challenge to the vaccine, the FDA said only the new BioPort batches can be used. In June, the Pentagon had ordered both the old and BioPort's newer vaccine to be used, in high threat areas only.

Because of the FDA's concession that the old vaccine, manufactured by the state of Michigan and sold by BioPort, was not properly tested for safety and effectiveness, Rempfer and Dingle said, the Defense Department should now promptly pardon hundreds of service members punished for refusing to be inoculated with that vaccine. They insist the department must properly care for the hundreds who became ill from adverse effects of the vaccine.

This is the shocking history of the anthrax vaccine on the Internet from Sherman Silversteing Attorneys at Law: https://www.sskrplaw.com/anthrax-chronology.html

As well, The National Vaccine Information Center is one of the most amazing Internet sites, supplying the basic descriptions of the anthrax vaccine and its health problems. Here it is: https://www.nvic.org/Vaccines-and-Diseases/Anthrax.aspx

It was President George Bush (the younger to his presidential father, George H.W. Bush) whose regime faced the court ruling making the vaccine illegal.

"Responding to a request for a preliminary injunction made in court in May 2003 by a group of soldiers who opposed the shots, Judge Emmet G. Sullivan of the U.S. District Court in Washington ruled the anthrax vaccine must be considered experimental, since it has never been approved by the Federal Drug Administration for the purposes the Pentagon uses it -- to protect members of the U.S. military from a weaponized anthrax attack," says a Salon.com article. https://www.salon.com/2003/12/23/anthrax_22/

CHAPTER 16

PRESIDENT GEORGE BUSH TAKES US TO WAR

One day, I received an unexpected and exciting news investigative request from my long time journalistic friend, now a college professor, John Briggs. He had a very hot tip on the crucial rational for the United States to have been lured into Middle East war. It turned out to be President George W. Bush's far right religious beliefs.

Bush was raised in a protestant home moving back and forth between between the Presbyterian and Episcopalian faiths. However, in 1985, Bush had a change of heart. He quit habitual drinking of alcohol in part because of the inspiration of evangelical Billy Graham, "found God" and joined the United Methodist Church.

Because his belief was that Christ died and rose again over Israel, he became very upset with the threats that potential dangers in Iraq leadership were posing to that very Israeli country.

And those menaces to what he considered Christ's country not far away, helped convince him that was a crucial rational for the United

States enter a conflict with Iran's Saddam Hussein who possessed or was in the process of creating weapons of mass destruction.

Here is what John Briggs and I discovered from months of investigation and creating the accurate news story about what we believed had gotten little public attention. That concerned this country being sucked into a war that seems in various ways to never end.

Bush, Mideast Wars and End-Time Prophecy

By JP Briggs II, PhD. D., and Thomas D. Williams

t r u t h o u t | Special Report

Friday 29 June 2007

"Religious institutions that use government power in support of themselves and force their views on persons of other faiths, or of no faith, undermine all our civil rights. Moreover, state support of an established religion tends to make the clergy unresponsive to their own people, and leads to corruption within religion itself. Erecting the 'wall of separation between church and state,' therefore, is absolutely essential in a free society."

- Former US President Thomas Jefferson

President George W. Bush has become dangerously steeped in ideas of Armageddon, the Apocalypse, an imminent war with Satanic forces in the Middle East, and an urgency to construct an American theocracy to fulfill God's end-of-days plan, according to close observers.

Historians and investigative journalists following the "end-time Christian" movement have grown alarmed at the impact it may be having on Bush's Middle East policies, including the current war in Iraq, the ongoing Israeli-Palestinian crisis, the strife in Lebanon and the administration's repeated attempts to find a cause for war against Iran.

Many people are aware that Bush is "the most aggressively religious president in American History," as eminent historian Arthur Schlesinger Jr. described him, (Schlesinger, "War and the Presidency," 143) but most remain without a clue to what this actually means.

One piece of evidence is Bush's funneling billions of dollars to "faith-based" organizations. Faith offices making grants are now so widespread inside government agencies that federal watchdog officials have serious difficulties accounting for how much money has actually been spent. (Goldberg, "Kingdom Coming" 121).

Marvin Olasky, a devotee of end-time theology, designed Bush's faith-based welfare concept. See also Goldberg, "Kingdom Coming," 110.

Further evidence is the Bush administration's transformation of the military. Until complaints forced its removal, a religious recruitment video made by a group called the Christian Embassy appeared on the Department of Defense web site.

The video included interviews made inside the Pentagon with seven high-ranking military officers, congressmen, other federal officials and even the Christian Ethiopian ambassador to the US about their personal relationship with Christ.

Army Lt. General William "Jerry" Boykin made headlines in 2003 when he said he believed America was engaged in a holy war as a "Christian nation" battling Satan. Adversaries can be defeated, he said, "only if we come against them in the name of Jesus." Despite his highly publicized rhetoric, Boykin remains Bush's deputy undersecretary of defense for intelligence.

Beneath Bush's benign-sounding words, "faith" and "Christian," lies the deeper reality of the authoritarian, doomsday religious beliefs of the ministers and spiritual counselors that surround him, say experts. Officially he has been at pains to show an openness traditionally expected of an American president.

Typical is his assertion in a speech at a National Prayer Breakfast found on the White House website: "There's another part of our heritage we are showing in Iraq, and that is the great American tradition of religious tolerance. The Iraqi people are mostly Muslims, and we respect the faith they practice."

However, experts point out the particular brand of Christianity that permeates Bush's environment is anything but tolerant. For example, Bush's own personal minister, Franklin Graham, has called Islam "evil and very wicked." He has said, "Let's use the weapons we have, the weapons of mass destruction if need be, and destroy the enemy."

Respected journalist Bill Moyers says that for the religious figures around Bush "a war with Islam in the Middle East is not something to be feared but welcomed - an essential conflagration on the road to redemption."

Scholars calculate that the group, which religion author Lynne Bundesen has dubbed "end-time Christians," has up to 40 million followers. Though not all may fully subscribe to the doomsday theology, they are inundated with it in books, megachurches, and on Christian broadcasting stations that reach millions upon millions of the faithful and are almost entirely dominated by end-time preachers.

The messages come from "dispensationalists," who believe that true believers are close to the time of being "raptured," or drawn up into heaven by God, in the days before the final battles. They also emanate from various stripes of "dominionists" pushing to erect an American theocracy for the end-of-the-world wars against the anti-Christ. (Read "Who Are The End-Time Christians?")

Crosshairs Iran - an Illustration

A potent example of the influence of end-time Christians in the White House developed in early May 2007 when the president invited dominionist James Dobson and 12 or 13 other "family value" ministers for a special meeting.

They were called in to discuss the "disturbing threats Iraq, Iran and international terrorism posed to US, Israel and other democracies around the world.

Dobson is best known as the founder of Focus on the Family, an end-time lobby. Dobson opposes homosexual rights and abortion, and advocates the "submission of women."

He has backed candidates who call for the execution of abortion providers, and works to establish an American theocracy. Dobson was careful not to quote the president in his radio address.

He declined a Truthout interview request about his influential relationship with Bush, including what his radio broadcast said involved many meetings in the past with the president.

Dobson told his listeners that Bush "appeared upbeat and determined and convinced that his mission is to protect this great nation from those who have threatened us." He said Bush wanted "to let history be his judge for the way he has dealt with this crisis in the Middle East.... He laid out the challenge before us."

The meeting with Bush, said Dobson, inspired an entire week of his radio discussions on radical Islam's impact on America. He said the "general tenor and tone" of his session with the president emphasized "how we are living in very perilous times, and the future generations of Americans depends upon how we rise to that challenge today."

He continued: "Iran has promised to blow Israel off the face of the earth, and they have made no bones about that.... They fully intend to wage war with us. They will do it when they have the nuclear and biological weapons to do it."

On the same program, Dobson pointedly discussed the president and the Iranian "threat" with bestselling author and dispensationalist Joel Rosenberg.

Rosenberg is an end-time "prophecy expert" who claims he makes frequent visits to the White House to help them "understand what will happen next in the Middle East."

He informed Dobson's listeners that Iranian President Mahmoud Ahmadinejad - the latest in a long line of end-time anti-Christ candidates that recently included Saddam Hussein - is "telling people inside Iran that he believes that the end of the world is just two or three years away."

Dobson, referring to Ahmadinejad, said: "We didn't take Hitler very seriously either. I just see the parallel. The president, it seems to me, does understand this."

Divine Mission

From the beginning of his presidency, Bush's own messianic statements have been downplayed or dismissed by the mainstream press - uncertain of how seriously to take them and shy of offending the religious feeling of their Christian audience.

In "American Theocracy," historian Kevin Phillips, a former Republican strategist, explores the question of Bush's professed sense of "divine mission."

"I trust God speaks through me. Without that, I couldn't do my job," the president told a gathering in 2004.

Phillips concludes that "the president of the United States may for some years have wandered into what we could describe as a period of personal theocracy, and he may have shaped US policy in the Middle East around a personal and radical interpretation of the Bible." (Phillips, "American Theocracy," XLII)

Former House Majority Leader Dick Armey told the BBC World Service in 2002 that he believed the president subscribed to end-time prophecies when "the whole world goes through a difficult time during those days of Tribulation."

Stephen Zunes, Middle East editor of the Foreign Policy in Focus project, observes that "Iraq has become the new Babylon" for Bush. In biblical Revelation, Babylon is the "great whore" representing human sin and corruption that will be destroyed to allow Jerusalem's rise and Jesus's return.

In an unscripted moment talking to the troops in April 2007 - as Iraq descended into chaos and the Democrats pressed him to pull the troops out - Bush seemed to offer a view of biblical Babylon and prophetic Tribulations. He said of Iraq: "It makes me realize the nature of the enemy that we face, which hardens my resolve to protect the American people. The people who do that are not people - you know, it's not a civil war; it is pure evil. And I believe we have an obligation to protect ourselves from that evil."

Paul S. Boyer, professor emeritus of history at the University of Wisconsin-Madison and author of "When Time Shall Be No More: Prophecy Belief in Modern American Culture," said in a lengthy telephone interview: "That sounds very much like Bush, kind of inarticulate, but also the workings of his mind are pretty clear. In his first speech after 9/11, he said he would rid the world of evil, which was an extreme evangelical sense of defining the war on terror."

Norton Mezvinsky, a distinguished CSU professor of history at Central Connecticut State University, has also extensively researched the Christian end-time movement and is writing a book on the subject.

In an interview in his office, he agreed the president's statement fits with his 9/11 pronouncements. "You knew Bush was saying, he just got the message from God; he finally realized why he was president of the United States."

Mezvinsky says, "There's no question that he is and has been influenced by the end-time ideas.... So there is a danger. To what extent? We don't know. The extent that we know is pretty bad."

A spokeswoman for the White House did not respond to nine requests by email and telephone for the president's answers to a series of questions about that influence.

But when Phillips's "American Theocracy" came out in March 2006, a questioner at a Bush speech referred to the historian's book and asked whether the president believed in the Apocalypse.

The Washington Post reported that Bush stammered and laughed nervously as he responded: "The answer is - I haven't really thought of it that way.... The first I've heard of that, by the way. I guess I'm more of a practical fellow."

Phillips writes in the new introduction to his book that Bush then went on with his answer for "four and a half minutes without ever mentioning the Apocalypse, Armageddon, the end-times, or the Book of Revelation." (Phillips, "American Theocracy," XL).

The Israel Connection

One of the most influential end-time Christian ministers with entree to the president is John Hagee.

Recently, Hagee updated his book, "Jerusalem Countdown," to highlight a coming war with Iran. It promises: "There will soon be a nuclear blast in the Middle East that will transform the road to Armageddon into a racetrack. America and Israel will either take down Iran or Iran will become nuclear and attempt to take down America and Israel."

Hagee claims Iran is producing nuclear "suitcase bombs." In 2006, Hagee assembled a large number of end-time Christian groups into an umbrella organization, Christians United for Israel. When (CUFI) met for the first time in Washington, Israel had just invaded Lebanon.

The British Telegraph newspaper reported that Hagee's "claim of political clout is no idle boast. The president sent a message of support praising him for 'spreading the hope of God's Love and the universal gift of freedom.'"

During the invasion period, www.raptureready.com, the website for those anticipating ascension into heaven before the final battles, excitement mushroomed. Responders thought the war in Lebanon signaled the start of the Tribulations. "This is so exciting," one commentator offered. "I have been having rapture dreams and I can't believe that this is really it! We are on the edge of eternity!" said another.

Meanwhile, other websites noted the curious echo of prophecy from a statement by Secretary of State Condoleezza Rice that clearly grated on foreign diplomats' nerves: "What we're seeing here are the birth pangs of a new Middle East," she said, even as she refused to call for a cease fire to end the killing and destruction going on in Lebanon.

The echo was a core prophetic verse in Matthew: "And you will hear of wars and rumors of wars; see that you are not alarmed; for this must take place, but the end is not yet. For nation will rise against nation, and kingdom against kingdom, and there will be famines and earthquakes in various places: all this is but the beginning of the birth-pangs."

Was it a coincidence of language from a woman who has described herself as born again and evangelical? Rice denied any such reference.

Though they give different, sometimes changing "literal" versions of how close the Apocalypse is, end-timers all agree that the establishment of Israeli hegemony over the biblical lands and the rebuilding of the ancient Jewish temple are preconditions for Christ's return.

From this belief derives the unwavering support of end-time Christians for Israel. Both dominionists and dispensationalists call themselves "Christian Zionists." End-time Christians (or Christian Zionists) have become Israel's main tourist revenue, shepherding groups to the holy land to see the sites of Armageddon and the Second Coming.

Mezvinsky has extensive contacts within the Israeli government and various conservative Israeli groups, and he is emphatic on one point: although a succession of Israeli prime ministers has courted the American end-timers (the Christian Zionists) and declared them Israel's "greatest friends," the Israelis don't accept the end-time theology one wit. They are also aware that it is anti-Semitic. (For one thing, they interpret the Bible as claiming that only 144,000 converted Jews will be allowed to survive the Apocalypse.)

However, Mezvinsky says, the Israelis also know that the end-time Christian Zionists are a lobby that can deliver US support for Israeli hard-line positions on arms, West Bank settlements, negotiations with the Arabs, and Iran.

Neocons and End-Timers

Historians Mezvinsky and Boyer stress that the power of blood-drenched, Satan-versus-God Christian prophecy has merged with another major factor shaping the Bush administration's Mideast policy and the current focus of hostility toward Iran.

As president, George W. Bush represents a perfect storm that has blown neoconservative ideology together with the end-time movement. Before 9/11, the neocons envisioned an American global empire supported by newly created democracies friendly to American interests in oil, markets and ideas. But they thought only a Pearl Harbor-type event like 9/11 would make mobilizing the country for it possible.

The key to this plan was the Middle East. Phillips says that designs on Middle East oil reserves, particularly in Iraq and Iran, were part of the neocon strategy. Notes Boyer, the neocons and end-timers "come at the subject of the Mideast war from different perspectives, but they end up agreeing."

In Bush's speeches, a careful coding of words and phrases also brings the neocon and end-time perspectives together. The president makes "liberty" and "democracy," for example, synonymous with "divine wishes." Read sidebar, "Hidden Behind Coded Language."

But Mezvinksy cautions that many neocon strategists probably think the end-time Christian Zionists "are nuts, but, boy, we can utilize them." Indeed, the thinly concealed disdain some neocons have expressed for the prophetic Christians has fed into the media habit of underestimating end-time influence on the assumption that only identifiable political ideas can shape policy.

Meanwhile, the influence of end-time Christians has burrowed deeply into the American Israel Political Action Committee, AIPAC, the powerful Israeli lobby. At the last AIPAC meeting with a long list of speakers that included Hillary Clinton and Barack Obama, "Hagee got the loudest applause of anybody," according to Mezvinsky.

Mezvinsky reports he is increasingly hearing Israelis say that "we want the United States focusing on Iran. Those are people who would like the United States to attack Iran. They realize that, given the involvement in Iraq, there's not the wherewithal to go after Iran." Israel Prime Minister Ehud Olmert has called Iran an "existential threat" to Israel.

This spring, AIPAC, with the help of its end-time supporters, succeeded in removing language from a military appropriations bill that would have required Bush to get Congressional approval before using military force against Iran. So again, Iran policy provides the example - here for how end-time religion, the politics of Israel and neocon strategies converge. And how end-time thinking entangles George W. Bush.

At about the same period that Bush was meeting with Dobson and Dobson was touting a war with Iran, Vice President Dick Cheney, the consummate neocon (no sign on his horizon of end-time religious views), stood on the deck of an American aircraft carrier just off Iran's coast. He warned that the United States was prepared to use its naval power to keep Tehran from disrupting oil routes or "gaining nuclear weapons."

But, a Cheney spokesperson cited his remarks on the aircraft carrier, as mentioned word-for-word on the White House Internet site, to suggest there is no warning to use naval power against Iran.

The Kuwait Times reported that Cheney had visited the region to forge an alliance among the United Arab Emirates, Jordan and Egypt "in support of a possible US strike against Iran over its controversial nuclear program, according to Jordanian politicians and academics." Cheney was apparently unsuccessful, the newspaper said.

When asked about his foreign policy position on Iran, a Cheney spokesperson cited a statement from Cheney: "We hope that we can solve the problem diplomatically. The president has indicated he wants to do everything he can to resolve it diplomatically.

That's why we've been working with the EU (European Union) and going through the United Nations with sanctions. But the president has also made it clear that we haven't taken any options off the table." The Cheney aide's references to Cheney statements made no mention about "a strike on Iran."

For probably different reasons, the fascination of Bush and Cheney for war with Iran has been longstanding. Reports say Secretary of Defense Donald Rumsfeld's original war plans for Iraq included moving on to Iran within 90 days of securing Baghdad.

The plans were later dropped, but they suited both neocon adventure for oil and democratization and the violent Christian prophecy that sees defeat of Babylon as a vital step on the path to the return of Christ. (Dubose and Bernstein, Vice 182) Through it all, nuclear bombs convey the awe of an Apocalypse.

In the spring of 2006, Pulitzer prize journalist Seymour Hersh reported Bush had ordered his generals to begin planning for an air assault on Iran's nuclear facilities using "bunker-busting" tactical nuclear weapons.

When generals tried to remove the nuclear option from the plans, they were "shouted down," Hersh wrote. Said a former senior intelligence official, "Bush and Cheney were dead serious about the nuclear planning." There were also reports the administration was trying to convince the Israelis to do the bombing.

Then in late February this year, new word came on Bush's Iran war planning. The London Times reported: "Some of America's most senior military commanders are prepared to resign if the White House orders a military strike against Iran, according to highly placed defense and intelligence sources. Tension in the Gulf region has raised fears that an attack on Iran is becoming increasingly likely before President George Bush leaves office.

The Sunday Times has learned that up to five (US) generals and admirals are willing to resign rather than approve what they consider would be a reckless attack. 'There are four or five generals and admirals we know of who would resign if Bush ordered an attack on Iran,' a source with close ties to British intelligence said. 'There is simply no stomach for it in the Pentagon, and a lot of people question whether such an attack would be effective or even possible.'"

In May 2007, the Inter Press Service reported that Admiral William J. Fallon, who was slated to become the Central Command chief on March 16, had sent a message to the Defense Department in mid-February, opposing any further US naval buildup in the Persian Gulf.

The news article said Fallon squelched an administration effort to send a third carrier strike group to the Gulf. That would have brought the US naval presence up to the same level as during the US air campaign against the Saddam Hussein regime in Iraq, the report said.

It continued: "A source who met privately with Fallon around the time of his confirmation hearing and who insists on anonymity quoted Fallon as saying that an attack on Iran 'will not happen on my watch.' Asked how he could be sure, the source says, Fallon replied, 'You know what choices I have. I'm a professional.' Fallon said that he was not alone, according to the source, adding, "There are several of us trying to put the crazies back in the box."

Of course, no one knows if the administration will eventually attack Iran. But experts believe that end-time ideas are playing a part in Bush's thinking about a widening war in the region.

End Game

Bundesen's sources within the religious community and in the military around the president tell her that end-timers are "crawling all over the White House and Camp David." These are men who purvey what Hedges calls a "theology of despair" that "feeds dark fantasies of revenge and empowerment."

Bundesen says she is not being cynical when she observes that end-time ministers like the late Jerry Falwell, Pat Robertson, John Hagee, Tim LaHaye and James Dobson have used their dark theology to increase their followers, pump up their power and fill their coffers.

And it's clear that Bush, in turn, has used end-time Christian leaders and their ideas for political and moral support. So isn't it just about politics?

No. Experts say that whether anybody even believes the violently apocalyptical scenarios shouldn't obscure the stark fact that Bush's policies have emerged in an atmosphere saturated with these dark ideas. Journalist Ron Suskind reported in 2004 that the administration prided itself on not being "reality-based," and the end-time vision may be one way to understand what that pride is about.

CHAPTER 17

GOVERNMENT CORRUPTION REQUIRES TOUGH JOURNALISM WORLDWIDE TO HELP CONTROL IT

The absolutely destructive atmosphere created by the corrupt leadership of any country, as it continues, can expose just how crucial it is to have a free press with sufficient finances for regular in depth and obviously fair news stories. Check what a close examination of leaders worldwide to discover how many have been, or are, seriously corrupt without serious public, news media or governmental challenges.

And, the incredible corruption, continuing daily, monthly and yearly within President Donald Trump's dark regime, proves how significant a fair, honest and in-depth news sites for newspapers, television or elsewhere can be. Check out countries around the world with widespread corruption and poor leadership. Then, analyze the qualities of their news! Truly wonder: has anyone ever done that?!

My emotional concerns about that decline of journalism inspired me to write not only this book, but as well, an in-depth news story about that very negative Trump regime subject in 2006. It was just a year after I retired from those decades of work as a Hartford Courant reporter and began my freelance investigative reporting work. That story appeared again later in other publications like this one.

See http://cooljustice.blogspot.com/2006/11/decline-of-journalism.html

To quote the lead paragraph: "If some doomsday industry analysts are to be believed, newspapers are laid out and stacked neatly inside their own future death warehouses, not only in the United States, but worldwide."

Now in with summer moving in by June 2020, after reading and viewing scores of news stories about the possible renewed attempts to impeach Trump, I'm happy to be a retired newsman!

My emotional concerns about that decline of journalism inspired me to write not only this book, but as well, an in depth news story about that very negative Trump regime subject in 2006. It was just a year after I retired from those decades of work as a Hartford Courant reporter and began my freelance investigative reporting work. That story appeared again later in other publications like this one.

See http://cooljustice.blogspot.com/2006/11/decline-of-journalism.html

To quote the lead paragraph: "If some doomsday industry analysts are to be believed, newspapers are laid out and stacked neatly inside their own future death warehouses, not only in the United States, but worldwide."

But the major professional news question of the latest time in history is: are newspapers, magazines, television and other news operations professionally handling one of the most crucial scandals worldwide: the investigation and impeachment of President Donald Trump?

His eventually predicted impeachment by the House's Democratic majority was always expected to be an eventual loss resolved by the dominance of Trump biased Republicans in the U.S. Senate. Indeed, the Senate's ruling to clear Trump, arriving relatively quickly, without Republicans allowing any witnesses at all, cleared President Trump.

How could it be that the Senate's impeachment trial, by law, did not mandate witnesses?! That's because earlier the U.S. Supreme Court ruled 9 to 0 in President Richard Nixon's legal case that no trial is required for the Senate to acquit, or convict, anyone impeached by the House of Representatives. But, fortunately, Nixon resigned before an impeachment hearing was begun.

A dramatic and shocking example of cursory news was the 2016 presidential election. The two major party candidates, Hillary Clinton and Donald Trump, created numerous scandalous controversies about one another, prompting scores of daily news articles. But, overall nationwide, relatively few timely in depth or investigative pieces appeared to effectively help scores of voters clarify scurrilous circumstances, charges and counter charges.

Can anyone imagine what would have happened had repeated reporting investigative pieces and follow up news appeared in newspapers BEFORE the election about Trump's scandalous sexual behaviors with at least two women, or his multiple business flops?

Other series of unrelated in-depth probes, mostly from The New York Times and The Washington Post, largely became most intense AFTER Trump was elected president in November 2016.

Following his win, President Trump seemed to even dream about restraining in depth and investigative reporting probing his alleged tight before and after election connections to
Russian President Vladimir Putin and the Russian's massive illegal sneak blog support for him.

In early October 2017, MSNBC quoted the president as saying, '' Why Isn't the Senate Intel Committee looking into the Fake News Networks in OUR country to see why so much of our news is just made up-FAKE!" And he texted at one point, eight months earlier, in February 2017: "THE FAKE NEWS media (failing NY Times, CNN, NBC news and many more) is not my enemy, it is the enemy of the American people. SICK!"

But when January 2019 came along, President Trump indeed became closely tied to a series of confidential conversations with Putin.

"A Washington Post exclusive revealed: Citing 'current and former U.S. officials,' the Post reports President Trump has a 'pattern' of hiding those (Putin) conversations from government officials and that he has, at least once, taken his interpreter's notes and told them not to discuss a conversation with administration officials.

These actions have reportedly led to a lack of details about five of the president's face-to-face communications with Putin over the last two years." https://www.newsy.com/stories/washington-post-trump-hid-details-of-putin-conversations/

As reported in EAWorldview, here is part of that very situation:

"After a one-on-one session with Putin at the G20 summit in Germany in July 2017, Trump took the notes of his interpreter and instructed that very person not to discuss the encounter with other Administration officials. The officials learned of Trump's order when a White House adviser and a senior State Department official sought information from the interpreter beyond a readout from Secretary of State Rex Tillerson."

"US officials said there is no detailed record, even in classified files, of Trump's face-to-face interactions with Putin at five locations over the past two years."

But even as much as revealing are these news reports of volunteer discussions in The New York Times January 20 and 21, 2019 editions from Trump's well-known spokesman-attorney, Rudolph W. Giuliani.

"President Trump was involved in discussions to build a skyscraper in Moscow throughout the entire 2016 presidential campaign, his personal lawyer said on Sunday, a longer and more significant role for Mr. Trump than he had previously acknowledged."

"The comments by his lawyer Rudolph W. Giuliani indicated that Mr. Trump's efforts to complete a business deal in Russia waned only after Americans cast ballots in the presidential election."

Soon after Giuliani was reported in The Times saying his comments about that proposed Trump Tower in Moscow were "hypothetical" and not intended to convey facts.

The reported new timetable means that Mr. Trump was seeking a deal at the time he was calling for an end to economic sanctions against Russia imposed by the Obama administration.

He was seeking that Russian deal when he gave interviews questioning the legitimacy of NATO, a favorite talking point of Russian President Putin. And yet, contrarily, on the other hand, he was seeking that Trump Tower deal when, in July 2016, he called on Russia to release hacked Democratic emails that Mr. Putin's government was rumored at the time to have stolen.

Meanwhile then, reportedly, U.S. Special Counsel Robert S. Mueller III was seeking witnesses to Trump's sensationally controversial confidential conversations with Putin, some of which were covered up by Trump's seizing of the minutes of those very discussions.

Other of those conversations were not recorded or texted into minutes available to U.S officials. They have led to speculation that Trump is somehow under Putin's control as a result of his overwhelming approval of his and Russia's controversial international policies, mostly directly opposed to U.S. policies.

Trump's intensive critiques of the press, excluding his longtime favorite biased Fox News, has continued from day one of his life in the media going back to his days in business and continuing overwhelmingly ever since.

Back in October 2016, The Washington Post quoted Trump as claiming: "Our press is allowed to say whatever they want and get away with it. And I think we should go to a system where if they do something wrong....I'm a big believer, tremendous believer of the freedom of the press. Nobody believes that stronger than me.... But, if they make terrible, terrible mistakes and those mistakes are made on purpose to injure people, and I'm not just talking about me, I'm talking about anybody else, then yes, I think you should have the ability to sue them."

 Indeed, Trump wanted stricter libel laws like those in England.

"Well in England they have a system where you can actually sue if someone says something wrong," Trump said. "Our press is allowed to say whatever they want and get away with it. And I think we should go to a system where if they do something wrong -- I'm a big believer, tremendous believer of the freedom of the press, nobody believes it stronger than me -- but if they make terrible, terrible mistakes and those mistakes are made on purpose to injure people, and I'm not just talking about me, I'm talking about anybody else, then yes, I think you should have the ability to sue them."

See CNN Business News: http://money.cnn.com/2016/10/24/media/donald-trump-sue-news-organizations/index.html

Trump wanted to change the libel law for politicians like him. The Digital Media Law Project says, that law is stricter for "celebrities, politicians, high-ranking or powerful government officials, and others with power in society (because they) are generally considered public figures/officials and are required to prove actual malice. On the other hand, a private figure is only required to prove negligence if you publish something defamatory about (them)."

Controversial in depth and investigative stories often appeared late in the 2016 presidential contest. They were delayed enough that their impact on opposing candidates and the public, and even more important, undecided voters, came too late for intelligent decision-making.

The national press reported a number of in-depth exposes, critiquing Mr. Trump, but the many of the most effective and powerful ones appeared AFTER he won the primaries and the presidency.

The controversial probe of Trump for his and his election promotional team began in May 2017 after allegations surfaced that they were suspected of teaming with the Russians to influence the presidential election on his behalf.

Here is the Wikipedia summary of it: "The ongoing Special Counsel investigation is a United States law enforcement and counterintelligence investigation of any Russian government efforts to interfere in the 2016 presidential election, including an investigation of any possible links and/or coordination between Donald Trump's presidential campaign and the Russian government, 'and any matters that arose or may arise directly from the investigation.' "

"The scope of the investigation reportedly also includes potential obstruction of justice by Trump and others. The investigation, since it began May 17, 2017, has been conducted by the United States Department of Justice Office of Special Counsel, headed Mueller, a former Director of the Federal Bureau of Investigation (FBI). Mueller took over several existing FBI investigations, including those involving former campaign chairman Paul Manafort and former National Security Adviser Michael Flynn."

That investigation has resulted in dozens of indictments for federal crimes, including charges leading to guilty pleas by Manafort and Flynn who have since agreed to cooperate with Mueller's and his team's investigation along with other crucial witnesses who also have been charged and plead guilty.

The probes of Trump, himself, have worked closer and closer to Mueller's obvious but confidential aims at implicating the president himself.

The most controversial of scores of investigations pointing to possible Trump criminal activities came in February 2019. That was when his former lawyer-confidant Michael Cohen began more of his testimony in Congress and supplied checks used for payments of Trump's sexual activity with Stormy Daniels, an adult film porn star.

The investigative effort was aimed at possibly leading Mueller to refer Trump to the U.S. House of Representatives for an investigation, but that never happened. If concluded unfavorably for him, would have moved Trump on to a trial in U.S. Senate. But it would have required even then, as previously mentioned, two thirds of the senators' votes with biased Republicans dominating, to remove him from office.

But, after that probe had been ignored by the House, another severe problem developed for President Trump when the Trump-Ukraine scandal began in September 2019. That began with the revelation that an intelligence officer had filed a whistle-blower complaint to the intelligence community inspector general alleging wrongdoing on the part of Trump.

The whistle-blower, a member of the CIA, claimed and detailed to the National Security Council, about a phone call in July 2019 between Trump and Ukrainian President Volodymyr Zelensky. A recording of it later revealed Trump sought to press Zelensky to dig up damaging information about one of his leading Democratic presidential challengers, former vice president Joe Biden.

That pressure included Trump's temporary unexplained decision to withhold a Congressional grant of hundreds of millions of dollars in military support as Ukraine they faced off against Russian aggression.

That led to a House of Representatives investigation and hearings resulting in Trump's impeachment for illegal activities with a foreign government to attempt to severely knock out his 2020 presidential rival candidate, former Democratic Vice President Biden.

The Senate, after refusing to allow the Democrats and the Republicans any witnesses, Trump, as a result of the overwhelming Republican majority in the Senate, was ridiculously cleared. Immediately, he loudly attacked Democratic senators and Republican Sen. Mitt Romney, the ONLY Republican to vote to impeach him, soulfully for abuse of power but not for obstruction of justice.

The press reported Romney's vote was the first time in US history that a member of the president's own party voted to convict and remove him from office. Indeed, two days before that vote, Romney predicted what he would do.

Here's what the Washington Post quoted Trump as saying after he learned of that vote against his continuing as president: "Mitt Romney never knew how to win. He is a pompous 'ass' who has been fighting me from the beginning, except when he begged me for my endorsement for his Senate run (I gave it to him), and when he begged me to be Secretary of State (I didn't give it to him). He is so bad for R's!"

He suggested it was Romney, himself, who should have been impeached, but didn't say for what!

As well, Trump fired several members of his staff called as witnesses who testified at his House impeachment, which I believe appears to be illegal, but immediately and initially was not publicized as such in The New York Times.

I wondered why these witnesses could be fired without civil or criminal probes against Trump and wrote the New York Times and House Impeachment leader Rep. Nancy Pelonsi, but received no answers or have observed no publicized activity. There was soon been a call for the illegality of this by at least one federal official and those outside the government.

"CNN Legal Analyst and former federal and state prosecutor Elie Honig says Trump's actions are "criminal." SEE https://www.thenewcivilrightsmovement.com/2020/02/friday-night-massacre-experts-says-trump-firing-of-3-officials-including-sondland-and-vindman-is-criminal-offense/

Trump not only had Lt. Col. Alexander Vindman transferred out of the White House, but he had him fired from his National Security Post and escorted out of the building. Vindman's twin brother, who also works on the NSC, was summarily fired and escorted out as well, as The New York Times reports.

If that were not enough Trump then turned around and had his Ambassador to the European Union, Gordon Sondland, fired as well.

Both Vindman and Sondland had testified before Congress, proving a now famous unidentified whistleblower's claims that the president engaged in disturbing behavior by extorting Ukraine. The General Accounting Office substantiated that claim, stating that Trump's withholding of hundreds of millions of dollars in military aid was illegal.

CNN Legal Analyst and former federal and state prosecutor Elie Honig says Trump's actions today are "criminal." says a news story.

Calling it a "Friday Night Massacre," professor of international relations and visiting professor at Johns Hopkins University, journalist, and CEO of The Rothkopf Group, David Rothkopf also says Trump's actions today are criminal. SEE https://www.thenewcivilrightsmovement.com/2020/02/friday-night-massacre-experts-says-trump-firing-of-3-officials-including-sondland-and-vindman-is-criminal-offense/

Generally, Trump and his allies have launched regular attacks on other GOP members who've criticized the president, part of a broader effort to keep rank-and-file members in line.

Most recently, in February, Trump has been pushing for leniency for Roger Jason Stone Jr., Trump's eldest political advisor, an American political consultant, author, lobbyist. He was convicted on seven counts, including witness tampering and lying to investigators. On January 25, 2019, Stone was arrested at his Fort Lauderdale, Florida, home in connection with Robert Mueller's Special Counsel investigation, involving Trump's corrupt activities.

After Trump in other earlier hot controversies, suggested on the White House lawn that China investigate former vice president Joe Biden and his son Hunter, Mitt Romney, the former Republican presidential candidate in the 2012 election., denounced the president, after Trump was cleared of impeachment in the Senate. He was one of the very few of any Republicans anywhere to be so critical.

Here's Romney's detailed opinion.

"When the only American citizen President Trump singles out for China's investigation is his political opponent in the midst of the Democratic nomination process, it strains credulity to suggest that it is anything other than politically motivated," Romney tweeted. "By all appearances, the President's brazen and unprecedented appeal to China and to Ukraine to investigate Joe Biden is wrong and appalling."

Only one other GOP senator beside Romney has criticized Trump's behavior, Nebraska Sen. Ben Sasse.

"Hold up: Americans don't look to Chinese commies for the truth," Sasse told the Omaha World-Herald. "If the Biden kid broke laws by selling his name to Beijing, that's a matter for American courts, not communist tyrants running torture camps."

But Sasse was careful to critique Democrats too. In the same interview, he said House Intelligence Committee Chairman Adam B. Schiff (D-Calif.) was "running a partisan clown show in Trump and Romney have a long, complicated history.

Trump's opinion of Romney used to be temporarily different. In 2012, Trump, who pushed a birther conspiracy theory about President Barack Obama, publicly endorsed the former Massachusetts governor Romney for president.

But after Romney's loss to Obama, Trump derided Romney's performance.

Romney actually outperformed Trump in the popular vote during their different years' primaries, winning 47.2 percent of the vote in 2012 to Trump's 46.1 percent in 2016. But unlike Trump, Romney failed to win enough states to secure an electoral college victory.

Romney was critical of Trump during the 2016 campaign, calling him a "phony." But Romney broke bread with Trump after he won the presidency. At the time, Trump was considering Romney for secretary of state.

When Romney won his Senate seat in 2018, he promised in an op-ed published the night before his swearing-in that he would stand up to Trump as needed, though until October 2019 now he has stayed mostly on the sidelines.

Romney was the sole Republican to vote for Trump's conviction in the Senate's impeachment final.

"His vote did little to change the all-but-guaranteed end to the president's impeachment trial — acquittal — but it dramatically shifted the surrounding narrative. An impeachment process that Trump had called entirely "partisan" no longer was so," NBS News reported.

As Democrats praised Romney for his act of "moral courage," Trump world began relentlessly attacking him. This heavy political and crucial dispute gives the concerned reader why these significant queries regarding Trump are essential for caring reporters and newsreaders.

APPENDIX

(JP Briggs II, D. is a Distinguished CSU professor at Western Connecticut State University, specializing in creative process. A former reporter for the Hartford Courant and coordinator of the journalism program at WCSU, he is currently senior editor of the intellectual journal "The Connecticut Review." His books include "Fire in the Crucible" (St. Martins Press); "Fractals, the Patterns of Chaos" (Simon and Schuster), and "Trickster Tales" (Fine Tooth Press), among others. Email: profbriggs@comcast.net.)

BOOK'S AUTHOR BIOGRAPHY

Thomas "Dennie" Williams is a former state and federal court reporter, who in addition specialized in investigations, for the Hartford Courant. Since the 1970s, he has written extensively about irregularities in the Connecticut Superior Court and the Probate Court systems as well as in depth reporting regarding disciplining both judges and lawyers for misconduct. One series of in-depth probate court stories by Dennie and Mark Stillman helped lead to the first impeachment of any official in state history. Dennie has additionally probed and written countless articles on the many failures of the Pentagon and the VA to assist sick veterans returning from war. His retirement came after over three decades of Courant reporting. Upon leaving The Courant, Dennie became a freelance reporter and has written scores of letters to the editor of several newspapers. (He can be reached at denniew@optonline.net.)

www.ingramcontent.com/pod-product-compliance
Lightning Source LLC
Chambersburg PA
CBHW060832220526
45466CB00003B/1071